HOW I MADE MILLIONS
IN REAL ESTATE AND
HOW YOU CAN TOO

JAMES EDWARD GLASGOW SR.

How I Made Millions in Real Estate and How You Can Too

Disclaimer and Legal Information:

The examples and anecdotes used in this book are designed to illustrate the opportunities, issues, and problems that you might encounter as a real estate investor. They may not portray any specific people or situations.

This book contains the opinions, ideas and methods of the author. It is intended to provide helpful and useful information on the subject of real estate investing as addressed in the book. It is sold with the understanding that neither the publisher nor author is engaged in rendering legal, accounting, tax, or any other kind of professional advice or services in this book. The reader should consult his or her tax adviser, accountant, real estate or legal professional, or other competent professional before adopting any of the concepts or ideas of the author or making any investment. The concepts in this book are specific to the investment made or are general concepts, whereas each reader's real estate investment opportunity is unique and specific to them.

The author and publisher specifically disclaim any and all responsibility and/or liability for loss or risk, personal or otherwise, which may be incurred, directly or indirectly, as a consequence of the use and/or application of any content of this book.

Visit us on the Web at www.BGPublishingInternational.com

Published by BG Publishing International
1304 SW 160th Avenue, Suite 203, Sunrise, FL 33326

Cover and Page Design by Perseus-Design.com

ISBN 978-0-936977-03-4

DEDICATION

To the memory of my mother, Alice Burning Glasgow, who passed on to me her love of books for the knowledge they contained. She believed that God has given us all an unlimited capacity to learn and that we should not waste this God-given gift.

My mother taught me that the word "can't" should never pass from my lips, as that word is a lie that declares defeat before one has even begun.

CONTENTS

INTRODUCTION

rich (adj.) Possessing great wealth, abundance.

Years ago, one of my daughters came home from school and asked me, "Daddy, are we rich?"

"Well, let's see," I replied. "You grew up with a lot of things that you consider normal, such as your own TV, VCR, phone, car, checking account, and credit cards, as well as birthday parties, pool parties, summer trips, all your school activities, new clothes, going out to eat and the cinema most weekends, getting a job at one of my businesses, etc. So, yes, a lot of what you consider to be normal is viewed by others as the luxuries of being rich. "You have these things because your parents work hard and choose to provide them."

I went on to explain that her responsibility was to be thankful for what she had, make the best of her life and its advantages, and never treat others as if she thought she was better than they were. Family, friends, and health, I said, are what truly make one rich. Everything else can be replaced.

"So, we're rich."

Yes, I said. We are.

There are 8,600,000 households in the United States that possess a net worth in excess of a million dollars.[1] Most people decide that someone is rich based on outward appearances: fancy cars, big boats, large houses, estates, ranches, airplanes, and tropical locations. If your goal is to have the trappings of the rich and famous, all you need is a large monthly cash flow.

Cash flow is just what it sounds like: the flow of money, in and out. As a real estate owner and landlord, I collect rents, I make my monthly payments on my mortgage notes, and I shell out for any necessary repairs. If I have money left over at the end of the month (or year), I have achieved a positive cash flow.[2]

Decide what you think rich is, and that will define your long-term goal. One definition is to have enough cash flow coming in each month to handle all of your obligations with enough left over to do those things you truly wish to do, without much consideration as to the cost of doing them. People consider me (and my family) to be rich because my monthly cash flow provides the trappings that people see as the purview of the rich.

When I turned 30, I had to acknowledge to myself that I had not reached my goal: I was not a millionaire yet. I realized that acquiring a million dollars was not a realistic goal and that it would keep me feeling depressed, a failure, if I did nothing more than give myself more years to reach a specific dollar amount.

If you had a million dollars in a bank CD, you might get $50,000 a year in interest. I would rather have a million dollars' worth of real estate making me $50,000 a year. Why? Because I can borrow the million dollars I need to control (purchase) the real estate—I don't have to have it. If you work on getting the monthly cash flow, getting rich will take care of itself.

---

[1] Frank, Robert. "Millionaire Population Grows by 200,000." *The Wall Street Journal.* 30 Oct. 2012.

[2] Gallinelli, Frank. *What Every REAL ESTATE Investor Needs To Know About CASH FLOW.* New York: McGraw-Hill Companies, 2009.

This book contains the motivation you need to start, the information, the knowledge, and the tools that you will need to be successful, and a bit of inspiration to keep you moving forward on that road toward a financially richer life.

Building wealth requires putting information and capital to work, combined with time and effort. Each method of investing money, each type of business, will have its own specific rules and requirements, but *the general rules of good business apply to ALL methods of making money.*

This book will provide both information and motivation. It will provide to you the trade secrets. It will reveal to you what works, so you do not have to learn the hard way or spend too much time doing it. And it intends to point you in the right direction.

As I discuss the different aspects of "thinking rich" and getting rich, I will use examples to illustrate the principles and make suggestions on how you can teach yourself the habit of "thinking rich."[3]

The rest is up to you.

---

[3] The names of all individuals, other than my own, have been changed to protect their privacy.

CHAPTER ONE

DECIDE TO BE RICH

Getting ahead is easy; so few people are really trying.

Gathering information, reading all the books you can, studying, learning, and talking about making money are all important. You must do all of these things, but taking action—**formulating a plan and acting on it**—is the only way you can make yourself rich.

If you are not moving forward toward wealth, you are losing ground. If you feel you are standing still, just working at your current job, without gaining the knowledge you need to acquire cash flow-generating assets, then, in fact, you are not standing still—you are losing ground. The cost of living and inflation are relentlessly eating away at your current assets.

The rich are always moving forward; they (or, more accurately, their investments) are always at work. That is the real reason why the rich get richer and the poor get poorer. You have to give yourself *permission* to be wealthy and then take actions every day that are designed to lead you toward wealth.

There are currently 314,677,986 people living in the U.S. today.[1] Millionaires make up only 2.7 percent of Americans. While that is certainly an increase from the year 2000, when only 1.3 percent of our population comprised millionaires, I still think the number is low. I believe this for two reasons: people aren't revealing to the government the true scope their assets; and people don't really understand the true value of their assets.

If people do not know what their assets are worth, this raises the question: Are those assets being used to their fullest potential? Probably not! How could they be? It has been my experience that getting ahead is not as difficult as people think. The reason more people do not get ahead and become rich is because there are so few people trying.

What this means is that there is not a lot of competition to prevent you from getting rich. The toughest competition you have is *you*. To get where you want to be, you must overcome procrastination and fear of success.

The toughest competition you have is *you*

For those of you who have been wasting your time and money on "get rich quick" schemes or spending your life working at a job that makes someone else rich, it's time to focus your energies on a plan *that works for you*. Many of us have already done so. You can be rich, too.

Top Ten Percent

If you have an adjusted gross income of $112,124 per year, you are in the top 10 percent of taxpayers in the U.S.[2] That is an interesting statistic.

[1] "U.S. and World Population Clocks." *United States Census Bureau.* 30 Oct. 2012. U.S. Department of Commerce. 30 Oct. 2012 < http://www.census.gov/main/www/popclock.html >.

[2] McCormally, Kevin. "Where Do You Rank as a Taxpayer?" *Kiplinger.* 30 Oct. 2012. 20 Sep. 2012 < http://www.kiplinger.com/article/taxes/T054-C000-S001-where-do-you-rank-as-a-taxpayer.html >.

It means that 90 percent of the people filing tax returns have an AGI of less than $112,000 per year. By using the information provided to you here in *How I Made Millions in Real Estate and How You Can Too*, you will be on your way to taking your place among **the top 5 percent—** the rich in America.

The average net worth of senior citizens has dropped from $199,000 to $170,494.[3] That's right. According to 2009 median figures, the average 65-year-old American's net worth is only $170,494. With Social Security and a little pension, they could still conceivably get by okay when they retire. I personally would rather have a million dollars or more by age 65 and have my home paid for so that I can live in a little more comfort than just merely getting by.

How about you?

Are you going to end up with that average amount of $170,494 at age 65? Or are you going to join me and the other wealth builders and be a millionaire instead? If you haven't joined us, do so now. If you have joined us on this road toward wealth, then stay motivated and reread these chapters until you know them so well that you can act quickly, assured that you know what you are doing when opportunity knocks.

What makes successful people different is how they choose to spend their days.

When I was twelve years old, my family worked the fields as migrant workers. We would start in Arizona, chopping the weeds out of cotton fields, and move on to the valleys of California to pick raisin grapes, followed by lettuce, and so on. One year, we were outside of Fresno,

---

[3] Wang, Jim. "Median Net Worth by Age." *Bargaineering.* 30 Oct. 2012. 20 June 2012 < http://www.bargaineering.com/articles/median-net-worth-age.html >.

California, picking raisin grapes. This involves picking and filling a large dishpan of grapes and spreading them out in a single layer on trays of craft paper to dry in the sun. The pay was seven cents per tray. It was hot, dirty work, complicated by spiders, snakes, and lizards.

One day, I was eating my sandwich while sitting near the foreman, who was clean, neat, and well rested. I asked him what his job entailed.

There are two types of people in this world: workers and bosses

Hiring workers, arranging for transportation and water, and paying workers on behalf of the farmers, he said. He made a percentage according to the work done. I asked him how one could get his job and, with a chuckle, he told me what to do. That was the day I realized that there were two types of people in this world: workers and bosses. The boss was the one who made the most money. I quit the next day and started my first business, picking grapes on contract.

From then on, I have always tried to be the boss. It was actually easier than you might think, as so few people were trying—or wanted the responsibility. The same is true of making money. Everyone talks about it, but so few actually get out there and do it.

Get-Rich-Quick Schemes

I did a search on Google using the words "making money" and I got back more than 1.14 billion hits in 0.49 seconds.

Most of those websites wanted to sell me a little booklet or tell me an easy way to make money with almost no effort on my part. I would bet that 99.9 percent of the people who try those get-rich-quick schemes fail. Most of those likely get discouraged and give up, or try another get-rich-quick scheme.

Of all the rich people I have met during the past forty years, not one has made their money by way of a get-rich-quick scheme. If you are looking for an easy way to quickly make a lot of money with little or no risk, you are in for a lot of heartache, and this is not the book for you. If making money were so easy, everyone would be doing it. If that person with the magic, secret way of getting rich really has that magic, that secret knowledge, why would they need you?

Making money takes work, time, investment, and knowledge. Millions of people all over the world are making themselves rich, and you can, too. The good news is that it is easier today to get rich than ever before. The bad news is that it still takes effort, time, money, and knowledge, with the emphasis being on effort and knowledge.

Prerequisites to Getting Rich

The pursuit of riches throughout the ages has been the driving force in the advancement of civilization. Mankind has prospered from these pursuits. The results were achieved by an energy that knew no bounds, by an unyielding human spirit that laid a foundation of prosperity over temporary failures.

If you practice the habits of continuous learning, accumulation of skills, and increasing knowledge, coupled with the traits and habits practiced by wealthy people, you will lay a firm foundation of true prosperity. Everybody admires the courageous spirit who overcomes difficulties and rises to the occasion.

To succeed, you will need to acquire these traits and habits—study, learn, and, most of all, put them to use as you move down your own road toward wealth.

The Traits and Habits of the Successful

Desire

If you truly desire to become rich, if you want it so much that it becomes an obsession, nothing will be able to keep you from achieving your goal. You must want it so badly that, if you go broke, you will start again. If your spouse is a hindrance, admit that you have chosen the wrong spouse. Desire wealth so much that you will not associate with those who have negative attitudes. It is this obsession that will allow you to build upon your failures, to work long hours; and it is this obsession to be rich that will drive you to pile up one success after another.

Positive attitude

Smile. It is the only way to start the day. My number two pick on this list is positive attitude, right after desire. Recently, I was talking with a financially well off, 80-year-old lady who'd had both knees replaced with artificial ones. Imagine the pain, the recovery, the physical therapy sessions, and the inconvenience she has weathered. Her comment to me was, "Look at the marvelous things they can do today! Isn't it great?" I can understand how she accumulated her wealth.

Confidence

Self-confidence is that unshakable belief that you are deserving, and that you will succeed in that which you set out to do. There is no defeat, except from within.

Perseverance

This is steadfastness, tenacity—that ability to stay with it until you succeed, to find another way, to overcome any obstacle. There are no insurmountable barriers except weakness of purpose. You must be firmly resolved to overcome any hindrance, that you will clear any difficulties from your path. Success does not come uninvited, and must be won with effort. Do not associate with those who see the glass as half-empty.

Planning

You must formulate a plan and put the plan into action. **Plan the work, and work the plan,** as they say. If you think of all that you have achieved so far in life, you will come to realize it was done by plan—maybe not your plan, but someone's.

In high school, your school had a plan by which its students would graduate four years hence: it had a time line, a sequence of events, and goals to be achieved as each student went along. The plan was flexible— you could choose some parts of it while others were set for you. All the requirements of a good plan were there. It had a time line (four years), it had a step-by-step method (you had to take ninth grade classes before tenth grade classes, for example), it had flexibility (if you stumbled, you could make the work up during the summer and, if you got ahead, you could add extra activities or classes that interested you.)

The school's plan was measurable (tests and grades), and you knew when you succeeded (graduation diploma). To be rich also takes a plan—and it is entirely up to you to do the planning and implementation.

Patience

You must have patience. Get-rich-quick schemes do not work. Decide which road(s) to wealth you will take and allow enough travel time. The next five years will pass, whether you start down that road to riches or not. So, get started! Starting now will make time your ally. For example, if you choose to own rental income properties as your road to riches, it can take years for the mortgages to be paid down, for rents to rise and property values to increase. That spread of time between the shrinking mortgage balance and increasing property values is what makes you rich.

Optimism

The rich tend to have a positive outlook on life. The rich see the glass as half full. Dwell on what you have to help you get richer and not what you think is lacking. Rich people tend to look at each situation to gain an understanding of how it might enhance their wealth or improve their life. Avoid associating with those who always take the path of least resistance.

Opportunism

When someone presents you with a problem, do you search for the positives? Or do you dwell on the negatives? When the stock market is down, do you focus on the loss in your portfolio's value or do you see an opportunity to buy low? Rich people keep their financial house in order so that, when an opportunity comes along, they are ready to take action. They find opportunity because they look for it.

Risk taking

Rich people tend to take calculated risks. When I am talking with wealthy people about risk, they describe themselves as risk averse. But when they tell me how they got where they are, it is almost always from having taken calculated risks. They are not averse to all risk, simply reckless risk.

For example, I know a dentist who takes the profits from his practice to purchase discounted secondary real estate loans (second mortgage notes) that return him 14 to 20 percent per annum. I know a landlord who retired after working 20 years with an auto parts company and who is so conservative that he keeps his cash in bank Certificates of Deposit (CDs). Yet, he has accumulated 22 rental homes (trailers) over the last 20 years. They bring in $12,000-plus per month in rents and he does not consider them risky at all. These professionals both accepted risk in areas in which they felt comfortable, and neither considers his ventures risky.

Honesty

The rich people I have met were straightforward and honest. I got the impression that they felt the best deals were those deals in which both parties were enriched. For the most part, I find rich people to be good, honest folks. Personally, I find it easier and a far better use of my efforts to be honest and not worry about what dishonest deed might come home to roost when I least expect it. Honesty breeds honor.

Education

Most rich people are educated in the subject areas they need to be in order to accomplish their goals. A formal education is not a prerequisite to getting rich. Many rich people have lacked university degrees. You need only to know where the library is, where the bookstores are, and how to make your way around the Internet. There is more information at your fingertips today than in the history of the world. The point is: *rich people never stop learning.*

Punctuality

Be on time! Being on time is the prelude to confidence. If you are habitually late and forever making excuses, you certainly won't exude confidence. Be a person of your word. Say what you mean and mean what you say.

Punctuality is a way to win friends and influence people. Punctuality also applies to returning calls or answering mail. Keeping anyone waiting is a mistake that you will unknowingly pay for.

Self-reliance

Do not rely too much on the advice of others and shun those who are mostly negative. Think for yourself. If the numbers work and the risk-reward tradeoff is acceptable to you, do not let all those timid souls talk you out of it. Surround yourself with like-minded friends with similar goals and ambitions. Only five percent of the population will become rich. Do not listen to the other 95 percent. Independence will add vitality and inspiration to your labors. If you let fear dominate, it will keep you poor.

Good credit

You need money to get rich. The good news is that *it does not have to be your money*. You must have A-1 credit. A good credit rating is your number one asset. Your access to the capital markets increases as you go down the road to wealth. The more assets and cash flow you accumulate, the more access to capital will be made available to you. That is why rich people tend to be older versus younger. If I went broke tomorrow, I could rebuild, as long as I maintained my stellar credit rating.

Resilience

Each person of means that I have met has told me of the failures they have had. It is most interesting to hear them speak of these failures, for they do not dwell on the details of the failure itself, but rather what they learned from it. They invariably tell me of how they took the ruins of that failure and turned lemons into lemonade. *Build on your failures— they make for a strong foundation.*

Luck

Rich people are lucky. I once purchased a three-bedroom, two-bath home for $15,000 and sold it six months later for $37,000. I cannot tell you the number of people who commented to me on how lucky I was to find such a sweetheart deal.

Interestingly, not one of those people asked me how I got that lucky. In actuality, I had been passing out business cards that declared, "I buy houses" for about a year and had evaluated more than a hundred homes before I stumbled across that fixer-upper bargain. You make your own luck.

Rich people are lucky because they work at it.

Good reputation

If you practice all the maxims listed here, you will garner an excellent reputation and deals will tend to come your way.

It is not what you say but rather what you do that becomes your mantle.

To summarize, the rich folks I have met were all self-confident, knew they wanted to be successful, trained themselves to recognize opportunity, and acted on those opportunities in their own individual ways. If I had to choose one thing that makes successful people more successful, it is that they are prepared to **take action** on an investment opportunity when it presents itself. The most important thing they do is to **get started** without hesitation and work at it relentlessly.

At the end of each day, ask yourself: "Did I take steps today toward reaching my goals?"

No one selects you to be rich. Only you can do that.

CHAPTER TWO

WHAT ARE YOU AFRAID OF?

All great people throughout history took the path least traveled.

When I ask people why they haven't started working toward getting rich, they don't usually have an answer. If I persist with the question, they say: "I don't know how," or "I'm afraid I'll fail." When I try to get them to be more specific, they cannot.

"I don't know where to start."

Investing seems so complicated and overwhelming. We are all afraid of the unknown. Most people fail to get rich because they never learned how. No one taught us about getting rich, not our high schools, not our colleges or universities. Rich people learned how to get rich by modeling their parents or were self-taught. If they were lucky, they had a mentor.

Most of us would hesitate to take action ourselves in a medical emergency. We would look for help. We would call for a doctor or paramedic. The difference between you and your doctor is that the doctor has been through an intensive, on-the-job supervised training program (internship), in addition to his years of schooling, to learn how to respond effectively to such emergencies with confidence and speed. I think we can agree that, with the same training and education, you could become a doctor, too.

It's the same with making money. If you knew what to do and when to do it, you would have the self-confidence to use your resources to become rich. Treating patients and making life and death decisions has got to be scarier than investing for your future. So, what are you afraid of?

Overcoming the Fear of Investing

To overcome the fear factor, let's take the problem apart so we can better understand what it is we are really dealing with.

Emotion

One problem is that, when dealing with money, we tend to get emotional. Money is an integral part of our daily lives. How do you reduce the emotional effect when making your investment decisions?

Separate investments from personal accounts

Rich people consider money used for investment or for business as separate from personal or household money. You instinctively do that already. At work, ideally when you are spending the company's money, you handle the situation much more carefully and without emotion *because it is not your money*. The same is true for borrowing money. Borrowing to make money is a different decision than borrowing for a personal purchase.

The first is a decision based on factual data and probabilities; the second is an emotional decision.

I have my money separated into three segments:

1. Personal accounts (e.g., checking and savings);

2. Long-term savings accounts (e.g., IRAs and annuities); and

3. Investment accounts (with each investment separately accounted for).

My family views the investment accounts as businesses, because they are. Separating the money helps get rid of the emotion associated with money.

Fear of the unknown

I overcame my fear of the unknown by choosing one area of investing and studying up on it. I chose single-family rentals (including duplexes), as my starting point. The first house I bought was on Dickson Street in San Antonio, Texas. After completing several of these types of deals, and my family saw there were no big disasters, our confidence grew, along with our abilities, and the fear went away.

Fear of loss

Depending on the type of investment you choose, there are appropriate methods to reduce the risk of loss to a reasonable level. This is called risk management and has become a major focus in the world today, with most companies and governments hiring risk managers and establishing risk management departments.

For example, in the area of real estate investments, implementing risk management means that you would do research, familiarize yourself with the area in which you are buying, buy quality properties, use good advisers, buy property and liability insurance, and so on.

For stock investments, you would research the companies whose stock you are considering purchasing, look for companies that pay dividends, buy quality stocks, and use stop-loss orders, all in order to reduce risk.

For mortgage investing, you would buy from a reputable broker and buy only first mortgages on properties located in good neighborhoods.

The trick here is to realize that *the risk of loss can be reduced*, thus putting the fear of loss into perspective.

What Have You Got to Lose?

Every quality investment type will have a means of reducing risk. You have to put your loss into perspective and realize the probability of loss is not likely to ever be or even near 100 percent, as long as you take a few precautions and do the research, the due diligence.

The following story illustrates that it's all in how you look at it.

Mary is 55 years old. She has been saving for retirement and has about $100,000 left in her stock portfolio and about $50,000 in home equity. She knows that, at her age, she has to do something to avoid a less than desirable retirement. She has been trying, using the conventional methods most people use, such as saving her money, buying mutual funds, etc. Then came the stock market slide and her investments shrank by half. Too many things were out of Mary's control—interest rates, the stock market, job security, etc. When you rely solely or too heavily upon things that are out of your control, diversification of investment funds becomes critical to your financial survival.

When I asked Mary what she intended to do, she replied, "More of the same, I guess." I reminded Mary that Einstein's definition of insanity was doing the same thing over and over again and expecting different results.

"Why not invest in other things?" I suggested.

"Like what?"

"What about real estate? Mortgages?"

"I don't know anything about them and I can't afford a loss." She was afraid, scared of losing all that she had worked for, afraid of not having enough now and ending up with even less.

"Mary, let's take a look at what you would be risking. You have $100,000 that is currently earning three percent interest, about $250 per month. By the time you reach age 62, the total you will have saved at that rate will be about $125,000.

Assuming a five percent yield when you retire, that amount of money will then earn you $6,250 per year, or $520 per month in retirement income. *That* is what you are risking. Now, what if you could be earning $980 per month right now?"

"How?" Mary was suddenly all ears.

"Let's assume you take your $100,000, plus another $30,000 from your home equity, and purchase a two-family house for $125,000 cash. Each unit should rent for about $700 per month, if not more." I was scribbling quickly, and showing her my figures. "That is $16,800 per year in income. Allowing for 30 percent to cover taxes, maintenance and vacancies, that would leave you $11,760 per year.

17

Over the next seven years, from now until you're age 62, that duplex would earn you $82,320. Let's ignore for now the fact that the original value of the duplex would increase, on average, about five percent per year and rental rates would increase a little also each year. At age 62, you would have about $232,320 in income and investment property value, plus any interest earned on the $82,320 income. I am assuming here that you would pay off your home equity loan (used to fund the downpayment) out of the money you are currently using to invest in your mutual fund each month."

"But, what do I do if the renters tear up the house?" Mary screwed up her face like she'd just tasted lemons.

"Okay, then let's look at that. What is the worst-case scenario that would not be covered by insurance? That they bust up the house and cause a few thousand dollars of damage? Say, $3,000 to fix it up? So, for one year, you only make $13,000 because of repairs—and you get to take a bigger tax deduction because of the loss incurred. The risk to reward is really small."

"What about dealing with the tenants? It feels like more than I'd be comfortable handling."

"You can make a deal with the renters to do their own minor repairs for a reduction in rent, or hire a real estate agency to handle the rental for you for 10 percent of the rent collected. What I do is start out by asking $50 more per month than I really want and lower the rent up to that amount if the tenants will handle minor repairs."

Mary looked thoughtful. "I hadn't considered that. It does sound better than what I'm doing now. When you describe the process, it doesn't seem scary at all."

"By paying cash you won't lose your investment, unless you fail to pay your property taxes or pay far more than the property is actually worth, and any appraisal will protect you from that happening," I pointed out. "The only risk you're really taking is the $250 your $100,000 is making for you today. What you are actually losing, by not considering all of the options, is the money that same $100,000 could be making. Your $100,000 could, over the next seven years, make five times what it's making now, with an active investment versus the passive investment you now have."

Now, Mary was smiling.

Lack of knowledge is the problem, not real fear. It was what Mary did not know that was making her afraid. All she had ever heard of was how terrible renters could be. She had never once talked directly to any of the myriad investors who owned all of those rental homes out in the world who have been getting quietly richer.

At age 62, Mary could sell the two-family house and have all the cash or, better yet, take the $82,000 rental income and buy another house for cash. She could get her rental income up to possibly $25,000 or $30,000 per year to add to her Social Security and pension from work. Investing like this, she most likely will be better off financially after she retires.

What are you really afraid of?

Failure? Losing cash? Looking bad? Appearing uninformed? I will tell you what scares me—being retired and not having enough money to enjoy it. Or, worst case scenario, having to depend upon my children or the government to take care of me when I should be enjoying my life after all my years of work.

What is stopping you? What is holding you back? Whatever it is, my advice to you is to overcome it. Get educated in your area of interest and take action to become rich. You did it once before in order to enter the work force. Do it again, this time for your future. Make educated decisions and you just might find yourself very well off. It does get easier each time you venture forth.

Each of us gets 24 hours each day. What have you done with yours today?

CHAPTER THREE

PLAN TO
BE RICH

"You can't hit home runs unless you step up to the plate."
~Unknown

You Need a "Get Rich" Plan

O nly five percent of the people in industrialized countries will get rich, and fewer in non-industrialized countries. (Currently 2.7 percent of the US population are considered to be rich.) That begs the question: Why aren't more people getting rich?

The answer is simple, yet complicated. The simple fact is that most people who want to be rich (and that's almost everyone) do not have a "Get Rich" plan, *and would not make the effort to implement a "Get Rich" plan if they did have one.* Most of us are unsure of ourselves and our abilities, and we do not give ourselves credit for being smart enough. Thus, we are fearful and uncertain. We fear ridicule and failure. Because of these fears, people never take the actions necessary to improve their circumstances and become rich.

Make a plan!

Educating yourself will help immensely, but the fear factor never entirely goes away, no matter how many times you do something. (Nor should it. It's a natural survival instinct, training you to avoid being reckless.) It is imperative that you find the strength to overcome your fear of taking action.

When I purchased my first rental property, I could hardly sleep at night. Years later, when I purchased a half-million-dollar office building and started to worry, I dug out my notes, reviewed my math to reassure me that I had made the right decision, and then went back to sleep. The difference was that, over those years, I had developed the skills to evaluate a deal and, as a result, trust my abilities. With knowledge and experience, we can overcome fear.

The Plan

You need a "Get Rich" plan. I like written plans as they force you to conceptualize and clarify your thoughts. A "Get Rich" plan is made up of several parts: a goal statement, a list of prerequisites, and a to-do list complete with dates. We'll discuss this in further detail in a moment.

Note that, if you are married and your spouse is not supportive, it may be more difficult to implement your plan, but not impossible.

Money

Let us get money out of the way right now. If you recall, back in chapter one, we discussed the prerequisites, the traits and habits necessary, to getting rich: desire, positive attitude, confidence, perseverance, planning, patience, optimism, opportunism, risk taking, honesty, education, punctuality, self-reliance, good credit, resilience, luck, and a good reputation.

You don't need money to get rich!

Having money is not a prerequisite to getting rich. Don't get me wrong—having money to work with helps, but it is not a prerequisite. The desire to be rich and a willingness to learn, combined with a calculated action plan as to how you intend to get there and a commitment to implement that plan are prerequisites.

I know many rich folks who started with no money and no family connections, including me. *No more excuses!* If you do not get rich in the next ten years, it is because *you chose not to try.*

Doubts

Up to this point, your mind is filling with doubts:

- I don't have any money

- I don't know where to start

- I have bad credit

- My spouse won't help

- I can't tell so-and-so—they'll think I'm nuts

- I don't have the time

… and so on. Yep, you're normal, all right! Among that 95 percent. The ones who choose not to be rich.

Sadly, we are surrounded by negativity. That's not entirely bad, as caution keeps you safe. But, if being rich is paramount, then you need to overcome negative, fear-based thinking and avoid negative people. You need to make thinking positively a habit. It's not easy to retrain your brain to think positively; you will need to work at it. Consider reading a classic on the subject, *Think and Grow Rich.*

In the meantime, try this. Make three Post-it® note signs that say *Think positively today!* and stick one on your bathroom mirror, one in your car (my car note covers my tachometer) and one on your computer screen (at work, or home, or both). Then, every time you say a negative thing or catch yourself thinking a negative thought, put a dollar bill in a jar marked your "Get Rich" savings account.

I started years ago by putting a quarter in my left pocket every time I had a negative thought and, at the end of the day, I poured those quarters into a jar I kept at home. The first month I had to skip lunch a few times because I had transferred all my money before noon to the left pocket.

This exercise teaches discipline, keeps you thinking about getting rich, and slowly changes your way of thinking. There's no better time than the present. STOP! Mark this page, set this book down and go make out your notes and post them in all those places I suggested. Remember, taking action is part of how to get rich.

Time

The next obstacle you will face is managing your time. Remember, there are no get-rich-quick schemes that work. Getting rich takes time. Most worthwhile endeavors do.

It takes time to plan, time to educate yourself, time to implement your plan, and time to make the plan work. Time will pass every day, whether you take action or not.

Do you manage your time or does the day slip away? How much time is wasted on the phone exchanging small talk when, instead, you could be implementing your plan or learning, researching, and/or thinking about ways to get rich? Take control of your time—it's a valuable asset, so invest it wisely.

The difference between the self-made millionaires and you is how they invest their time and use their minds. Every other difference between you and a self-made rich person is nothing more than an obstacle to overcome or an excuse for not implementing your own "Get Rich" plan. If you have a thinking and reasoning mind and you take control of your time, then the only thing standing between you and riches is *YOU*!

EXAMPLE

Betty is in her early forties. She has some experience managing a small business and understands accounting and time management. Betty has a burning desire to get ahead and is willing to work at it, although, as a single mother of four, both time and money are scarce.

Betty's Plan
To start an e-business, and then begin investing in real estate. Online retail fits in with my low budget startup needs and the upside potential means I can make a good income after a few years. I will rewrite this plan as the research is being done so I can create a step-by-step plan with a timeline.

GOALS
Within 60 days:

- Begin researching starting an online retail sales company

- Decide what to sell

- Order a name (URL) for the business

- Start setting up the business (at the end of 60 days)

Within six (6) months:

- Launch the website

Within 18 months:

- To be selling $50,000 per month, at which time begin working on it full-time.

Implementation Challenge

Betty has made a decision as to what she will do and a commitment as to when. Her biggest obstacle will be time. As anyone with four kids knows, spare time is a rare commodity. She will be up many long nights after the kids are in bed working on her new online business.

EXAMPLE

Mark and Sara are a middle-class couple in their mid-fifties. Sara is being downsized this fall and will receive a severance package. They do not save much; their income typically runs out before the month is over. She is not worried about finding another job and is also considering retiring early. Mark has no pension and will only have Social Security at retirement.

The goal is to get out of debt and subsequently make investments that will bring in extra monthly income so that, in ten or fifteen years, they can retire without worries.

Mark and Sara's Plan

In the next 30 days, we will design a plan to get out of debt and create an investment plan geared toward bringing in $2000–3000 per month in extra spendable income.

GOALS

Within seven (7) days:

- Make out a household budget

- Draft a personal financial statement

Within 30 days:

- Design a plan to deal with all debt after analyzing all options

- Construct a savings plan to start after debt is paid

- Begin learning about investing, so as not to rely on others; focus on rental real estate investing to leverage the limited money available; study other investment methods

Within four (4) months:

- Design "Get Rich," monthly income investment and implementation/ action plans

- Set aside severance pay to initially fund monthly income investment plan

Implementation Challenge

One of Mark and Sara's biggest challenges will be to train themselves to change their spending habits in order to start saving and pay down debt, instead of living paycheck to paycheck.

As you can see, a "Get Rich" plan is not difficult to put together. It is really more of a "Get Started" plan. You are setting out mile markers: where you are today, where you want to be in the near future, and where it is that you plan to get started, with a time control line. The first goal is to get started and form the habit of working at getting rich on a regular basis. "Get Rich" plans are vague on purpose. As you do your research and preparations, you will take notes, make revisions, and a more detailed plan will emerge.

You never stop planning—there is no point where you say, "Okay, I'm rich now, so I can stop planning and just let things take care of themselves." Rich people stay on top of their financial situation; they always know where they stand. You should continue to create a plan each year to accommodate your change in situation, in addition to any new challenges or considerations that may present themselves down the road.

As you accomplish the things in your "Get Rich" plan, your confidence will grow. The next plan you write will be more detailed and you will see your numbers growing. The following year, your personal financial statement will look even better. You will begin to have money left over at the end of the month after expenses. You will begin to save that extra money.

The next thing you know, you will be weighing a major household purchase against investing the money. When that day comes, you will have crossed the line. You will have developed the habit of thinking rich—go and celebrate!

Recently, I was considering getting a new truck because the one I had was older and gas is expensive. With $8,000 down, I knew I could afford the payments with ease. I paused. I thought about what else I could do with that $8,000. What if I drove the old truck another three years and used the $8,000 for a downpayment on a rental house?

I'll bet you can guess what I did.

The old truck was costing me $0.40 per mile for gasoline. The IRS lets me take a $0.54 per mile tax deduction for time spent managing my rental properties. Suddenly, that old paid-off truck I'd wanted to upgrade began looking a lot more attractive.

CHAPTER FOUR

PREPARING TO GET UNDERWAY

This one thing I do well, for it is my obligation to myself.

Cash-flow Rich

S ufficient monthly cash flow will allow you to live as if money is of little concern. Most rich people get their money from several sources: their job, investments, real estate holdings, tax savings, and business income. Every rich person I know uses a combination of these sources to produce a monthly cash flow that allows them to live as if money was of little consequence.

Don't Eat Your Children!

Once upon a time, deep in the jungle, there lived a cannibal tribe. In years when wild game was scarce, the families would eat their young children in order to survive. As the years passed, there came a time when the game stayed scarce for a prolonged period and they soon found themselves with no children left to eat.

The wild lions returned, and, as all the remaining tribal members were old and there were no young men to protect them, the lions attacked.

About 30 years ago, I read a report related to reinvesting some of what comes your way in order to make more.

It cited the example of two farmers who planted grain one year. The first farmer harvested his grain and sold every bit of surplus. The second farmer did the same, except that he saved a few pounds to use as seed for the following year. When it came time to plant the next year, the first farmer had neither the money to buy seed nor any seed to plant. The second farmer had the seed on hand to plant on time. He did not *eat his children.*

Now, the first farmer could admittedly just go out and get a loan in order to buy more seed to plant, but the extra time, cost, and problems could have been avoided with forethought. The moral of the story is always to set aside something for the future. For you and me, *Don't Eat Your Children!* means to be ready always to take advantage of opportunity when it comes our way.

Something magical happens when we do this. If we are financially ready to take advantage of profitable opportunities, if we have kept up to date with information concerning our area of interest, the more opportunities present themselves.

How do you make yourself ready?

- Budget carefully and save the extra money that comes into your household so that you are ready for any opportunities that come along.

- Set aside 20 percent or more of the profits made on any deal you make as "seed money" for the next deal.

- Maintain an excellent credit rating so that you always have access to money at competitive rates when you need it.

- Stay abreast of whatever area of interest you have so that you know a good deal when it is presented to you.

- Read those newspapers and journals applicable to your area of interest, whether stocks, bonds, real estate, development, REITs, or any of the hundreds of other ways of putting your money to work.

- Get started. Do a small deal to get your feet wet, and learn as you go.

The key is to be ready, both financially and mentally, to act when a profitable opportunity comes your way.

These five things are your children: the extra money you casually spend, the profits from the last deal you did, the credit rating that allows you to multiply your monetary assets, the knowledge that gives you the edge, if you possess it, and the stalwart attitude to act when you are presented with opportunity so as not to be numbered among the poor and timid souls who can only state: "If only I had had that back when..."

Don't eat your children! Only then will you be ready when opportunity strikes.

The Employee Who Wouldn't Work Overtime

In the 1970s, I was a clothing manager for a discount retailer, Globe, similar to today's Kmart or Target.

We had a very good, hard-working employee in the menswear department who I wanted to promote to department manager at a nice increase in pay. Every time I asked him to work overtime or work an extra day, he turned me down. Each time I asked him to consider the department manager's job, he said no. Finally, I asked him to have lunch with me and quizzed him as to why he was turning down the extra work and promotion.

He explained that his job was a means to his end. He needed a salary to show a steady income when applying for loans to buy houses. If he worked more hours to increase his salary, however, he would not have enough time to fix up the houses before the next payment would be due, and the lost rental income would be far greater than any overtime pay he could earn. He had seven houses by then, and, the day he got that number up to twelve, he was planning to quit his job at the store in order to work on his rental business full-time.

I never forgot that lunch.

I am a history buff. I like to study 19th century history in particular. What I have learned from business books of that era is that not much has changed since then in the business world. The skills and traits it took more than a century ago to get ahead are still needed today.

This advice is from a business book, copyright 1886: "Gain knowledge, maintain your honesty, be a hard worker, gain capital, have confidence, protect your integrity, practice perseverance, attend to your duty, be economical, avoid litigation, be polite and affable, be slow to anger, hone your skills, and be alert to opportunity."[1]

The only real difference today is that the speed of change has greatly increased and it has gotten easier.

Getting rich requires capital, information, and skill.

---

[1] "The Business Guide" by J.L. Nichols, 1886–1912, J.L. Nichols & Co., Naperville, IL.

It is actually easier today to get started than ever before. When I wanted to buy my first rental house, I first had to save up the downpayment. I needed a good credit rating and I had to prove to the banker that I could make the payments without relying upon the rental income.

The access to capital is much easier today. My daughter, at 19, has credit cards that would allow her to raise more than $10,000 and she is still in college with only a part-time job.

In the past, the competitive advantage the rich had over you was their access to information and capital. Today, that access to information, via the Internet, is at your fingertips at any hour of the day, and access to capital is readily available to anyone with good credit.

Today, all the barriers are down. There is no excuse left. True, it is easier to make money if you have money to work with but, if you have a good credit rating, then you have access to capital, and if you have an Internet connection, you have access to information.

Getting rich requires capital, information, skill, and knowledge. You must develop the knowledge and skills to effectively use your available capital and information. As you move down that road toward wealth and begin to accumulate moneymaking assets, your access to larger pools of capital will increase, usually in direct proportion to your skill level.

We are living in exciting times.

Making a Living

We all have to make a living, and it is difficult to borrow money without a verifiable source of income. But, times have changed and, for the most part, working for one company for 30 years until you retire is not a realistic goal (unless you are working in a government job with a solid pension).

You can work for yourself and control your future, or you can work for a corporation and hope that the job and your 401(k) continue to be there when you need them. As you must work to make a living, I will suggest another

Don't just work for a living

way of looking at your working career, one that I have used for the last 30-plus years.

Instead of working for a living, try working only where the experience will help you reach your long-term goals. Think of your place of employment as if it were a university. When you are no longer learning new things, you move on. You no longer care about pay raises or vacation time.

You are working for the experience and to be the best you can possibly be at the job. You are working for you, not for the employer. If you do this diligently, you will see a positive change in your attitude and your interaction with all the people you work with will be greatly enhanced. Your employer's and your fellow employees' attitudes toward you will change. After a few months of implementing this new outlook, your biggest problem will be turning down the inevitable pay raises and promotions, because they do not fit in to your long-term plan.

Formulate a financial plan detailing where you want to be in the next five to ten years. What path toward wealth have you chosen? Do you want to be a landlord? Importer? Internet retailer? Corporate executive? Manufacturer?

Put the plan in a written format with a lot of detail. For example, if you love to cook and would like to own an Italian restaurant in Dallas, Texas, plan this venture right down to the decor. The details you write down will tell you what you need to know in order to achieve the goal.

In the case of the Italian restaurant, you need to become a chef or very good Italian cook (or learn how to hire a good one). You will need to know restaurant bookkeeping and have business management skills. You will need to learn how to decorate the restaurant to attract the type of customers you wish to serve. You will need to learn the best way to lay out the floor plan of your restaurant in order to maximize revenue.

Since you wish to start the business in Dallas, Texas, then that is where you should be living. Get yourself a job in the nicest Italian restaurant in Dallas and work in all the different related job areas possible. Do anything and everything you can, from washing dishes to managing the restaurant.

Any time the people you are working for have you stuck in a job you have mastered and you feel trapped, quit and move on to another establishment. Be the best employee they ever had because you are really working for you and you deserve it. If you do this diligently, within two or three years you will be managing any place at which you work. If you are not, ask yourself why you are still there. In your spare time, take business classes at a local college and read as many books as you can about the restaurant business.

While you are working in these restaurants, you will meet suppliers, cooks, waitresses, bankers, investors, etc. These are the types of contacts who will prove helpful to you when the time comes for you to strike out on your own. Cultivate them.

Key Idea

Save up enough money so that you can live for three months without working. That nest egg will give you the freedom to quit any job any time you need to. Once you begin to look at a job as a means of accomplishing your goals, and you have the freedom (via your savings) to quit a job any time it is not helping you reach your goal, you will develop a new way of looking at your job and your work will become more enjoyable, because it's focus has become more positive—it's on you and your goals to get ahead.

This plan will work no matter what field you wish to enter (unless perhaps the field you choose has an advanced degree requirement that you don't presently meet).

Whenever possible, work for a monthly salary or on commission. If you are a person who likes getting paid by the hour, STOP! You are not rich material. I do not want or care to hear all the reasons you like being paid by the hour. They are all self-defeating.

If being rich is your passion, ask yourself this: Of all the people you know personally or publicly who are very well off (rich), or even well known, how many get paid by the hour? I'll bet the answer is NONE!

There is nothing wrong with being an employee. If being an employee is your desire, get the best job you can with the most benefits, one that suits your lifestyle. Save every penny you can in a 401(k), if you have that option. Then cross your fingers and hope that nothing goes wrong. Tens of millions of people are doing this every day and most survive.

But they don't get rich.

Borrow Yourself Rich

You can borrow yourself rich. It is not for everyone— you need lots of discipline and self-confidence. If you tend to be a procrastinator, this is not for you. It requires that you use your analytical abilities.

Borrowing yourself rich can best be explained as borrowing to purchase income-producing assets, properties, or businesses and using the income they generate to repay the loans. As the loan principal is repaid, you become a little richer each month.

Real estate is a safer bet. By using single-family homes as rental properties, borrowing yourself rich is fairly easy. I will assume here that you live in an area where reasonably priced houses are available. How can you tell if your area is priced correctly? Take the going rental rate for homes in the area in which you are thinking of buying and multiply the monthly rent by 100. Houses in that area should be selling for that amount or less.

We will discuss using real estate to get rich in more depth in the next section, *Riches through Real Estate*, however, let's briefly look at an example here of what I mean.

EXAMPLE

If the rental rate for houses in your area of the country is $1,100 a month, then the most you will want to pay for a rental house is $110,000. Include all related expenses, including all closing costs, of buying and getting the house into a rentable condition. I am going to make a couple of assumptions here to simplify this example. These assumptions are:

- You are financing 100 percent

- You are paying the closing costs out of your pocket

Let's look at the numbers.

- You buy a house in a ready-to-rent condition for $110,000.

- Monthly payments on a 30-year mortgage of $110,000 at 6.5 percent interest equal $695. Add monthly escrowed taxes and insurance of $225 and you have a total payment of $920 a month.

- Your rental income is $1100 a month, yielding you a positive cash flow of $179 a month.

To the positive cash flow you add the monthly principal payment portion of the mortgage ($90 of that $695) and your total return becomes $179 + $90 = $269 per month.

(At a seven percent mortgage rate, your payment would be $731 a month, reducing your cash flow from $179 to $143 a month.)

What if you purchased ten of this type of rental? In five years you would be $161,400 richer, not including the appreciation on the properties, any rental income increases, or the inevitable income tax savings. Chances are, the total return on your investment would be closer to $250,000, incorporating all those factors.

"I don't have enough for a downpayment."

Not a problem. The rule is: The less money you have, the more of your time will be required. The more money you have, the less time you will need to invest.

Ways to avoid a downpayment include: seller financing, buying repossessions directly from banks, pre-foreclosure takeovers, using other properties you own as collateral to borrow the downpayments, taking on partners who will supply the cash, trading other assets in lieu of cash, and lease purchase, to name a few.

I am simplifying things a bit, but the results are real enough. I ask you this: Where else can you get a part-time job with the potential to pay you $50,000 a year?

Want to make even more? Keep reading. All the information is here. This is real, and can be done.

Are you bold enough to do it?

Save Yourself Rich

You can save yourself rich. Given enough time, you can accumulate a million dollars or more by saving. The Rule of 72 states that you can calculate how long it will take to double your money by dividing the annual compounding interest rate by 72.

If you make an investment of $10,000 at 12 percent interest (divide 12 by 72), it will double every six years. At 10 percent it will double every 7.2 years, and, at six percent, it will double every 12 years. I used 12 percent for my example, as that is the historic long-term stock market return at the time of this writing. That $10,000 you have just invested will grow to $640,000 in 40 years, exclusive of income taxes and investment fees. So, find a 12 percent return in a tax-free investment vehicle and you are good to go ... well, at least you will be in 40 years.

I choose not to save money in the traditional way, such as a savings or retirement account. Yes, you can save yourself rich, if that is your choice. My only suggestion is that you start early and look for any method that will increase those savings rates.

Instead of having savings (I was never very good at saving through traditional means), I have developed enough monthly cash flow to do those things my family truly wants to do without worrying much about where the money will come from. If I had $3,000 lying around in a savings account, I would buy a rental house with it.

My brother-in-law has $750,000 in his company's savings account, accumulated over thirty years from monthly payroll deductions and his employer's stock purchase program. One day, some years ago, he asked me *how I managed to live better when he made more money.* I pointed out that we spent all of our paychecks and had no appreciable savings while he religiously saved some of his paycheck every month.

My brother-in-law uses his salary to save for retirement and to live on. I spend my paychecks plus some of the positive cash flow from my investments, giving me a higher standard of living while I slowly get richer because my tenants pay down my mortgages.

My brother-in-law may well save himself rich with the help of his employer's stock plan. I let my renters and businesses make me rich: same goal, different methods. In all my conversations with wealthy people, savings accounts were never discussed.

My brother-in-law has his money in a company-sponsored savings account earning low interest rates. I have my money working for me in investments and businesses. My money earns much higher returns than my brother-in-law's savings accounts and provides me with sufficient monthly cash flow to allow me to do what I want, when I want. That difference in approach can make a big difference to your standard of living.

CHAPTER FIVE

RICHES THROUGH REAL ESTATE

Make Millions from Real Estate

R eal estate is a huge market. Think about it. Everyone occupies real estate every day, and most people own some. In this section, I will share what I have learned in more than 45 years of real estate investing, some methods I use to value deals, and firsthand accounts of some of the deals I've done that will hopefully help you.

I will also cover some different methods of investing in rental properties, some of which you may not find in books, such as renting buildings without the land, trailer/mobile home home rentals with and without land, and how those people who put the signs up that say "We buy houses" operate.

We will touch on types of real estate investors, timing, closings, improving properties, secrets of real estate investing, options, profits, financing, notes, taxes, and much more.

Income-producing real estate is one of the best methods you can use to get rich. The best time to get started in real estate investing is when the economy is bad.

There are so many advantages to owning real estate as an investment that you should give it serious consideration, even if you do not plan to use real estate as your primary source of wealth building. Here are some primary advantages:

- Real estate generates cash income

- Real estate provides equity growth

- Tax advantages reduce your tax liability

- You can use leverage when financing the purchase

- Real estate protects you against inflation and deflation

You will learn even more ways to ensure your real estate investments make you money, if you keep reading.

If you plan on owning a small business, you will find that a lot of the value you build up in your small business over time will be in its real estate holdings. The borrowing power of your small businesses—and you as an individual—is greatly increased if you own real estate.

There are more advantages to investing in income-producing real estate than any other investment vehicle I can think of. There are some great books on real estate investing. While some may seem out of date, remember that the basics have not changed, only the tax laws.

Real estate helped make America great. The property ownership system and laws in the United States helped build this great country. Let me explain why.

I saw a PBS documentary on how, in most Third World countries, the quality of the governments, their laws, and their recordkeeping are so poor as to make it difficult, if not downright impossible, to prove who owns the real property. The inability to prove documented ownership makes it virtually out of the question to be able to borrow in order to finance a home or borrow against the real estate's value for any other purpose. This fact is one of the reasons people living in Third World countries have a hard time improving their lot in life.

Most people and small business owners in the United States have a large percentage of their savings tied up in their homes and in business real estate. They can readily access that savings by borrowing against their property or by selling it.

We are lucky that we live in a country where real estate is considered one of the safest investments available. You can use that trust in our system to help make you rich.

Advantages of investing in income-producing properties

Income or cash flow: A properly structured real estate deal can produce current income. That income increases as the value of real estate and rents increase.

Tax savings: The IRS rules and US tax laws allow you to take depreciation on the structures on a property. You can deduct the interest on the mortgage and the operating expenses against the income generated from the property. And, if you have a taxable loss, you can possibly use that loss to reduce your earned income. Other tax rules allow you to postpone taxes on long-term property gains.

Note: *Always keep your personal and professional funds separate. Deposit all money borrowed for investing purposes in a separate bank account. In order to deduct the interest on the borrowed funds, you will need to show the money was used for investments.*

Leverage: Using a small amount of your own money, you can borrow other people's money (known as OPM) to finance a property. By borrowing, you can control a larger property with a larger income stream than would be available from a smaller property for which you paid cash. Using other people's money is easier to do in real estate transactions than in virtually any other investment. OPM is used to finance the investment while the rents from the property pay down your mortgage, increasing your net worth over time.

Equity buildup: Each time a payment on the mortgage is made, assuming it's not an interest-only mortgage, which you want to avoid since the idea is to get richer by building equity, the principal portion of that payment increases your net worth. This is the essential magic of real estate investing: your money working for you while other people's (tenants) money is working for you.

Flexibility: There are many ways to buy, finance, control, and dispose of real estate, such as mortgages by the VA or FHA, seller-carried notes, purchase money mortgages or deeds of trust, wraparound mortgages, blanket mortgages, and rent-to-own deals, for example. (We will take a closer look at these vehicles further on.)

Appreciation: A properly maintained property will increase in value over time. The more desirable the area in which your property is located, the faster the appreciation will be. If an area declines, trade your way into a better area.

Inflation protection: Real estate has historically increased in value at or higher than the rate of inflation. Your property's rental income can be increased as prices, in general, increase, thus protecting your cash flow from inflation.

Readily available: Real estate is everywhere. But, as you have no doubt heard before, it's all about location, location, location. Happily, in addition to your own efforts, you have a whole industry waiting to serve your needs—agents, bankers, appraisers, even title companies.

Here is a link to *CoStar*, a very good commercial real estate newsletter: www.costar.com.

What Type of Real Estate Investor Do You Want to Be?

The first decision a real estate investor needs to make is what kind of investor they want to be. (This comes before finding the money and, obviously, finding good properties to acquire.)

Real estate investors most often specialize in one area of investing, and then add more areas as time, experience, or necessity dictates. For example, I started out buying rental houses for cash flow and long-term equity buildup. Years later, I became a mortgage lender, as I sold off some of those properties. Now, I both buy to hold and buy to sell, carrying the paper for my buyer, to generate cash flow.

As a real estate investor, you need to determine your area of interest. First, determine your investment goals and then decide which type of real estate investment will help you meet those goals and which type of investment suits your level of risk tolerance. In each of the investment areas listed below, there are subcategories, or specialties, as well as overlaps.

Types of Real Estate Investors

- Mortgage holder

- Short-term lender

- Landlord – cash flow investor

- Landlord – long-term equity gains

- Absentee landlord

- Dealer/flipper

- Tax lien buyer

- Equity partner with other investors

- Limited partner in a limited partnership

- General partner in a limited partnership

- Landlord – commercial

- Landlord – industrial

- Developer

- Landholder for future appreciation

- Land converter

Mortgage holder: Lender who finances the purchase of real estate for users or investors. Loans are secured by liens on the real estate and possibly with recourse against the borrower. This type of investor seeks interest returns reflecting limited risk. Returns typically average 7–10 percent.

Hard moneylenders seek returns closer to 20 percent. They take more risk, such as lending on properties with incomplete rehabilitation.

Short-term lender: Lenders who lend to flippers and for bridge loans until a longer-term, takeout loan can be completed. Returns are typically 20 percent-plus.

Landlord – cash flow investor: This is the most common type of investor. These investors buy property and expect a positive monthly cash flow from renting said property. The net spendable monthly cash flow is the primary concern. Equity appreciation, tax savings, and debt pay-down are secondary.

Landlord – long-term equity gains: These investors seek well-positioned properties to appreciate in value over many years. As long as the property pays for itself, they are happy. Their profits come from tax savings on the rental income, increases in value over time, rising equity levels derived from rental income paying down the mortgage, and rent increases over time. Returns can be as much as 20 percent annualized.

Absentee landlord: These investors buy ready-to-rent properties or properties already cash flowing that are professionally managed by rental management companies. Cash flow is the primary goal, with property value appreciation secondary. Returns are typically 8–12 percent per year. The properties can be located anywhere, as the investor relies upon real estate professionals to handle all aspects, from acquisition to daily management.

Dealer/flipper: Flippers find bargain-priced properties, often either fixer-uppers or those worth upgrading, and rehabilitate them for resale. Some flippers focus on finding below market value properties and then immediately resell them to other investors. Returns range from very good to none at all.

Tax lien buyer: Some states sell tax liens at auction. (Florida is one such state.) When people do not pay their property taxes on time, the county places a lien on the property. When the county needs operating cash flow, they sell the liens (debt) to investors. When the property taxes are paid or the property is sold, the lien is paid off and the investor gets his money back, plus accumulated interest. Returns average about 14 percent.

Equity partner with other investors: Money is the hardest part of the equation for most real estate investors. Because of this, many an experienced real estate investor will partner with an inexperienced money investor. The money investor gets a return on his cash, plus participation in the deal, while benefiting from his partner's experience. The experienced investor, on the other hand, gets the needed cash to do another deal. The more cash in a deal (versus borrowed money), the less risk. By taking on a money partner, an experienced investor reduces the risk in exchange for giving up part of the future profits.

Limited partner in a limited partnership: A limited partner provides a portion of the cash in a deal alongside other investors while the general partner assumes the management and borrowing risk. The cash investor's risk is limited to the amount of cash invested.

Check with your state as to the rules governing written agreements and tax consequences involved. It has distinct advantages, such as pass-through taxation, but each state, and sometimes districts within states, can differ as to legislation concerning how these companies are handled. Some lenders won't allow you to hold the property that secures their note in an LLC (limited liability company) or give you a loan on property already in an LLC.[1]

General partner in a limited partnership: A general partner in a limited partnership assumes all management and liabilities of the partnership. A general partner can also be a limited partner. The terms of the partnership, as indicated above, are governed by the limited partnership agreement and the laws of your state.

Landlord – commercial: Commercial property investors are those who prefer professional tenants. Contracts are longer, dollar amounts often larger, and the problems fewer. Downsides include the fact that vacancies tend to last longer and new tenants may demand remodeling allowances. However, returns are more predictable because expense

---

[1] Eldred, PhD, Gary W. *Investing in Real Estate*, 6th Ed., Hoboken: John Wiley & Sons, Inc., 2009.

increases can often be passed along to the tenants. Successful tenants tend to stay because the costs of moving can be steep.

Returns are typically 7 to 12 percent. The real estate investment return rate is often referred to as the cap (capitalization) rate, which is defined as the percentage or ratio of the net operating income versus the purchase price paid. (See Q&A section, "How much interest should I expect to pay?" for more on this calculation.)

Landlord – industrial: Similar to other commercial property investors, industrial investors study the market. Because industrial properties can be hard to lease after a tenant vacates, experience is essential to success. Potential for environmental liability further increases the risk.

Developer: A property developer looks for property that can be converted to its highest and best use. It might be a mini-storage or strip center, to name just two. The development process can be both expensive and time consuming. Returns can be very good upon resale, once a property is cash flowing.

Landholder: Some investors buy land to hold until a person comes along who needs it. Deep pockets are required because it can cost 5 to 10 percent a year in carrying costs to hold vacant land. These investors look to get out in front of an area's growth pattern and then wait for the city to catch up with it.

Land converter: These investors convert land to another use. For example, they might buy a ranch and subdivide it into smaller lots, or they might buy up several smaller adjoining lots to make a larger building site available to a developer.

Real Estate Investments by Property Types

There are advantages and disadvantages to different types of real properties.

Single-family home advantages:
Easy to purchase

Easy to rent

Easy to sell

Easy to finance

Flexible financing

Single-family home disadvantages:
High purchase cost compared to rental income

Single occupancy (vacancy) represents 100 percent of income

High maintenance costs

Duplex advantages:
Easy to purchase

Easy to rent

Easy to sell

Easy to finance

Flexible financing

Dual rent income

Duplex disadvantages:
High purchase costs compared to rental income

A vacancy represents 50 percent of income

High maintenance

Apartment (four or more units) advantages:
Per unit cost is lower

Easy to rent

Value is determined by income potential

Flexible financing

A single vacancy is a smaller percentage of total rental income

Apartment (four or more units) disadvantages:
Harder to finance

Larger downpayment

Harder to sell

Vacant land advantages:
Easy to purchase

High profit if in the correct place at the correct time.

Owner financing often available

Vacant land disadvantages:
Hard to lease

Hard to finance

High carrying costs

Lack of income

Hard to sell

High downpayment

Retail strip center advantages:
Easy to rent if in a good location

High rents per square foot

Low maintenance

Successful tenants tend to stay

Retail strip center disadvantages:
Hard to finance

A bad location is very difficult to fix

Larger downpayments

Vacancies can last awhile

Small office building advantages

Easy to rent if in good location

High rents per square foot

Low maintenance

Successful tenants tend to stay

Small office building disadvantages:

Hard to finance

A bad location is very hard to fix

Larger downpayments

Vacancies can last awhile

Small warehouse advantages:

Easy to rent if in good location

High rents per square foot

Low maintenance

Successful tenants tend to stay

Small warehouse disadvantages:

Hard to finance

A bad location is very hard to fix

Larger downpayments

Vacancies can last awhile

Other types of properties include farms, large office buildings, malls, large warehouses, factories, REITS, partnerships, and more.

Each of these has advantages unique to the type of investment; the biggest advantage is economy of scale. It is advisable to leave these types of investments alone until you become a more experienced investor, better equipped to assess the specific advantages and disadvantages.

NOTE: If you choose to start real estate investing by purchasing single-family homes, work hard to acquire more than one rental house as soon as possible, or keep a cash reserve in case of vacancy. When you have several rental units, your risk is spread out.

With just one rental house, one vacancy equals 100 percent, meaning zero income. With five houses and one vacancy, the vacancy rate drops to 20 percent.

With multiple rentals, the income from your other rentals will also offset any necessary outlay caused by a problem tenant. In all my years of investing in real estate, I have never experienced a mathematical loss of more than 10 percent of the overall real estate value, and, while I've occasionally broken even, I have never actually lost money on a deal.

Real estate is typically a longer-term investment

Real estate investing disadvantages in general: Real estate investments lack liquidity over the short term. Accordingly, if you need to sell fast, you could suffer a loss. It is not advisable to invest in real estate without some expert advice. Some degree of physical and mental effort is required to maintain a real estate investment, and there is always some risk that a property might decrease in value or the cash flow might not be sufficient to cover your carrying costs. To reduce this risk, it is imperative that you read and learn all that you can beforehand on the subject.

Ways to Invest in Real Estate

Methods to the madness

What makes real estate investing exciting is that there are so many ways to make a profit. There are properties available in every price range, for every person's pocketbook and investment style. Here, we will discuss a general description of some of the methods that people use to conduct their real estate investments. Often, several of these methods get combined into one deal, especially over time, as needs or opportunities change. There are no schools where the details of these methods are taught. We all learn as we go along. My purpose here is to stimulate your thinking and inspire you to learn more.

Dealer – buy, improve, sell

If you buy property for a quick resale, you are referred to as a dealer. Your goal is to buy low and sell high on a short-term basis. You are looking for bargains because you only make your money when you resell the property. As your goal is to sell the property quickly, the lower the price you pay, with the least amount down, the more profit and flexibility you have when it comes time to sell.

This requires finding houses that are undervalued, i.e., selling for less than the fair market price, or properties that would increase in value if they were spruced up a little. In order to succeed as a dealer, you need to study all you can about single-family home buying and selling. Read all the books you can. Gain a lot of knowledge about creative deal making. This knowledge will be invaluable to your success.

Ideally, you want to buy at 20 percent below the market price for a home needing cosmetic repairs and touchups. Try to buy homes financed by the seller with little down and no "due on sale" clause. As the subsequent seller, you want to offer financing (hold the note) and demand a larger downpayment than the one you provided, and carry the mortgage note at a higher interest rate than you are paying.

EXAMPLE

You buy a seller-financed home for $40,000, with $2,000 down, at 7 percent interest for 20 years, and with the first payment due in 90 days. You spruce the home up in short order and sell it for $50,000, asking $3,000 down, and seller-finance it at 10 percent interest for 30 years. You end up with your downpayment back plus 50 percent, and a positive cash flow on the equity difference between the two loan balances ($47,000 versus $38,000). You also gain a small amount of equity spread each month as the loan you used to buy the house is for a shorter term (20 years) than the mortgage you provided your buyer (30 years) when you sold the house. There are tens of thousands of deals out there that can be done this way.

Landlord – buy, rent, hold long term

This is the most common method of real estate investing. Here, you are looking for houses that will rent for more than your payments on the house. You goal should be to create a positive cash flow, to buy with the smallest possible downpayment and pay the lowest possible interest rate. Your profits will come from the positive monthly cash flow, increases in the rents over the years, the tax advantages due to the depreciation of the building, tax deductions on interest paid, the equity buildup as the mortgage is paid down, and the increase in the house's value due to inflation.

You may also gain from interest and tax advantages by selling the house years later and carrying the mortgage yourself. I have a house that I purchased 19 years ago for $32,000 on a 20-year note at $299 per month. I collected rent on it for 17 years (the rental income covered the mortgage) and then I sold the house for $40,000 at $365 per month on a 20-year note. My original purchase note will be paid off next year and the buyer I sold the house to will be paying me for many more years.

Distressed dealer – "We buy houses for cash"

We have all seen these signs. There is even a franchise available called "Homevestors." Here again, you are a dealer (in homes) rather than an investor. Quick turnover is where the money is. These dealers are looking for anyone wanting to sell a home quickly so they can get the house for a very low purchase price. Some of the reasons people are willing to sell homes at distressed prices include: homes in need of repair, back taxes due, divorce, death, fire damage, relocation, and some are just tired of being landlords. The dealer quickly corrects the deficiencies and resells the home.

In order to do this, you need to line up sources of quick cash by finding lenders, such as doctors, lawyers, business people, etc., who will let you have purchase money. Expect to pay very high interest rates, up to 24 percent and/or a percentage of the deal, or a flat dollar amount in addition to the interest. The reason for this is that you may only need the money for 30 to 90 days and even the high interest rates may not be enough of a profit to entice people to lend you this short-term risk money.

Once you obtain financing and buy the property, you fix up the home and put it back on the market, offering owner-financing. You will need another group of investors to buy the mortgage notes from you, or you can sell the notes on the secondary note market at a discount, or you can borrow against the note. Most of the lenders willing to buy notes on this type of property will want 20 to 25 percent annual returns. Your cost for funds will be high, and therefore you must buy the homes quite cheaply to cover all the costs and still turn a profit. This is a business rather than an investment and there is a lot you must learn in order to be successful at it. When done right, the profits can be very good.

Tax sale purchasers

Most counties hold tax sales of real estate on the courthouse steps. Property owners who fail to pay their property taxes may find their property auctioned off to the highest bidder. Notices are posted in the local commercial newspaper and on the bulletin board at the County courthouse. Special deeds are issued, and the property owners have reclaiming rights. (In Texas, the reclamation period is two years.)

Check with county offices for information on tax sales. Be sure to inspect the property beforehand and have a plan for what you will do with the property once the holding period for the original property owner to reclaim it has expired. When you see a house boarded up, chances are it was purchased at a tax sale and is being held in inventory, waiting for the former owner's reclamation period to expire.

Landlord – mobile homes

If maximum monthly cash flow is your goal, then renting mobile homes is better than renting houses. Buying mobile homes costs less than buying standard homes, and mobile homes can be put on smaller lots, thus, you can own more rental units for the dollars invested.

Every dwelling unit has a certain amount of shelter value, regardless of whether it is a house, a mobile home, or an apartment. Because this is true, the less you have to invest to provide that dwelling unit, the more profit you can make.

One of my friends has accumulated 20 mobile home rental units over the years and is installing six more this year. Here are the highlights of how he operates. All of the units are outside of the city limits near a school. All of the units are older units purchased for under $5000. He fixes them up just well enough to get them rented. He buys a piece of land where he can put three or more on the same property. He lets everyone know that he will buy a mobile home or land for cash if the price is right.

This year I watched him buy a 12 x 48-foot mobile home for $1500 and six lots for $12,000. By the time he gets the six lots set up with mobile homes and puts in the septic tanks, he will have invested about $100,000 for six rental units. If you consider a low rental rate of $500 per month, multiplied by six units, that is $3000 per month over twelve months, which equals $36,000 per year in rental income. That is a 100 percent return on his $100,000 investment in less than just three years.

The disadvantages are that the homes do not appreciate in value, and financing can be hard to come by.

Purchasers of buildings without land to rent

Here are two ways to do this. You buy mobile homes as cheaply as possible, rent vacant sites in mobile home parks, install the mobile homes there and rent them out. Because you do not own the land, your monthly profits will be decreased by the rent you pay for the lots. But this method does allow you to get started with less cash. Be sure the mobile home park owner is aware of your plans, and that the park's lot lease permits you to do this.

Another method is to lease out portable or prefabricated office buildings or storage units that you set up on vacant land that you have rented. Examples of this would be office trailers for long-term construction projects, school classroom buildings, church classrooms, guardhouses and backyard storage units, etc. This business requires cash to buy the units, and financing can be very hard to come by. The only effective way I have found to find the people needing to rent the buildings is to have a Yellow Pages ad that states you lease, for example, office buildings.

You will need sufficient cash to buy the buildings and must cut deals with portable building and/or office trailer manufacturers to buy at wholesale prices. I once leased four small, portable office buildings for a total of $775 a month. They had been leased to the same company for five years. The units cost me a total of $25,000, giving me a 32-month payback. A little over five years later, the buildings were sold to a tenant for $10,200. I collected a total of $61,350 on a $25,000 investment, a 145 percent return over five years, which, if divided by five years, yields a 29 percent return per year.

Undeveloped land speculators

Leave this one to the experts. The carrying cost of raw land is very difficult to overcome. If you can find a way to make the land produce income, then you can make a lot of money from raw land speculation. I own one piece of raw land and have it leased out as a mobile home sales lot. The property has been a very good investment for me. However, I had to carry it for several years at a large negative cash flow.

Landlords – commercial warehouses

These can be very good as a long-term investment. You find a piece of land where the access is good, but the location is slightly off the beaten track. You erect a four- to six-thousand-square-foot metal building with the minimum required office and restroom facilities. These types of buildings are popular with small businesses.

One of my businesses leases a warehouse of 4000 square feet for $1600 per month on a three-year lease. The landlady has so many of this type of property that her monthly gross income is $75,000. That is just shy of a million dollars a year. Her family has been doing this for over thirty years and most of the warehouses are paid for. I was so impressed with her operation that I have since added this type of real estate investment to my future "to do" list.

Commercial land speculators

This is another type of raw land dealer. They own or buy a piece of land where they think a need will exist in the future, and then they put up a sign that says, "Will build to suit."

Another method is to cut a deal with the landowner to put up such a sign on the condition that you will buy the land if you find a tenant. Here is a simplified description of the process: once you find a user who represents a very good credit risk, obtain a letter of commitment from them to lease the building long term if you build it to suit. When that's done, you obtain an option to buy the land from the owner and then secure your financing. Once you receive the loan commitment, you finalize the lease with your new tenant. Experienced investors usually do these complicated, cash-intensive deals.

Landlord – office buildings

Office buildings are often great investments if you have a little more money to work with and the staying power, should vacancy rates run high during a business downturn. The location and condition of the building will dictate the type of clientele you can attract.

Office space leases for about the same as apartments per square foot without requiring kitchens and bathrooms. As they are not normally occupied 24 hours a day, they often require considerably less maintenance.

The disadvantages are that they tend to be vacant longer, and it takes longer to resell the property. They also require downpayments approaching 30 percent. If you are buying the office building from which to run your own business, you can get an SBA-guaranteed loan with 10 percent down, and lease up to 49 percent of the space to other users.

Land developers

Land developers buy large tracts of land and develop the land into industrial parks, mobile home lots, or subdivisions in all their various forms. This is definitely an area where experience is important and large amounts of investment capital are needed. Most of these developments take years to get approved, and the projects can last for many years.

Lender – purchaser of mortgage notes

If you have a lot of cash to invest and seek high returns, buying mortgages may be for you. There is a very large market dealing in first and second mortgage notes. There are brokers who can find mortgages for you to purchase, and even manage the whole process.

Alternatively, you can search the mortgage lien filings in the county records and offer to buy notes from their holders. You can even call the people with those signs that say, "We buy houses." Some of them need buyers for notes. Contact any real estate investor club in your area for potential leads. It is possible to get a better than 20 percent return by buying notes at a discount.

For example, you find a note where the seller carried back a first lien on the home for $40,000 at 8 percent interest for twenty years. You offer the seller cash for 90 percent of the balance owed. The note holder gets $36,000 now and you get the payments, with interest, on the full $40,000, greatly increasing your return on the $36,000 you actually paid out. That would give you an annual return of over 14 percent on your $36,000.

Highest and best use purchasers

This type of investor looks for property potentially worth more should the use of the property be changed. Here are a few examples. You are limited only by your imagination and the local marketplace.

EXAMPLE 1

A house has one side facing a busy street and the front facing a side street. You check the zoning and confirm that it's approved for both residential and commercial use or that a variance is possible to obtain. You buy the house, convert the zoning to commercial, and rent it as office space.

EXAMPLE 2

An office building rents month to month and has attracted a less desirable type of tenant as a result. You spruce it up, add security, and switch to two-to five-year leases, thus attracting a better class of tenants at higher rates.

EXAMPLE 3

You buy a warehouse with adjacent land, lease the building, fence off the land, and rent it to companies looking for outdoor storage. For instance, you could rent to a company that rents barricades and needs a place to store them, or as a construction equipment storage yard.

EXAMPLE 4

You buy a mobile home park that rents its spaces to mobile home owners and convert it to one where you own the homes, thus getting more rent per space available.

Other types of real estate deals would include parking lots, buying large acreage and dividing it into small building lots that are sold on contract for deed, RV parks, outdoor storage yards, or flea markets, to name a few.

You can also invest in real estate through **real estate investment trusts** (**REITs**—see your stockbroker) or with real estate limited partnerships. Always check with your tax adviser first.

Ten Common Errors of Beginner Investors

The following are the most common errors made by beginning real estate investors. If you read this entire book, you will have what you need to tackle real estate investing. Practice what you read here, and you will be richer.

1. **Overpaying because you failed to crunch the numbers carefully**

   The property must have a positive cash flow. You have to be able to rent the place with enough to cover all of your monthly expenses and still have something left over. If you can do that, you can hold onto it.

2. **Underestimating the cost of repairs and the time it takes to do them**

   Keep in mind, everything always takes twice as long as you think it will and costs twice as much. *It is your total cost that determines whether you will make a profit.*

3. **Failing to check tenant credit and rental histories**

   This should be arguably rank at the top of the list, because bad tenants make renting a nightmare and good tenants make the place a cash cow. Charge prospective renters an application fee to cover the cost of credit, criminal, and rental history background checks and make sure you do them.

4. **Renting to relatives**

   In one word: *don't*. It is seldom, if ever, a pretty picture.

5. **Being nice to tenants who do not pay their rent**

If the tenant does not pay the rent, start the eviction letter process right away. I tell my renters that I am the nicest guy they will ever meet until they do not pay the rent; and then, I am one mean landlord—very mean. I will hold up my end of the bargain and take care of their apartment in a timely manner. I also evict non-payers in the same timely manner.

6. **Thinking you can do all the repairs yourself**

Hire someone unless you can do it right now. The faster the repairs are done, the better and cheaper it is. Your tenants deserve a nice place to live that is well maintained, and you deserve and must demand to get paid on time. They go hand in hand.

7. **Buying without considering selling from the very beginning**

You make your money when you buy and you realize your profit when you sell. The time to think about selling is while you are still considering buying the place. What will your buyer want to see? Will you be able to deliver that when you are ready to sell?

8. **Over-thinking the deal**

If the property works for you, if you feel you can make it pay, if the numbers work and you can do the deal, and you're hesitating, STOP! Stop thinking and buy it.

9. **Not maintaining the property**

I get my best bargains because landlords neglect their properties. That drives away the better tenants and keeps rents low. I simply buy at the current economic value, less the cost of repairs. I then do the delayed maintenance and raise the rents. And then I can sell at a profit. If you take care of your property, you do not give the tenant a reason not to pay the rent.

10. Not having a "What if?" plan

I have purchased properties under all kinds of circumstances, but I always have a "What if?" plan. If this deal takes six months to get the cash flowing, how will I make the payments? If my repair estimates are too low, what will I do to compensate?

You get the idea. I think of all the things that might go wrong and then I propose solutions. Having a "What if?" plan gets rid of the panic and makes it easier to decide whether to do a deal.

CHAPTER SIX

GETTING STARTED

Earned success arrives on each hour. Is this your hour?

I started my real estate investing with an owner-financed $28,000 house with a garage apartment. My most recent deal, at the time of this writing, was an office building requiring a $700,000 loan. My next project is a mini-storage that will involve a loan of about $2,100,000 and a total deal value of about $2,800,000. My point is that it gets easier to do larger deals as your financial statement and experience improves.

I will assume that your goal is to acquire a monthly cash flow by investing in income-producing real estate. I recommend that you start with an occupied two-tenant property to halve your vacancy risk. This section is about how to find that first property. By setting your sights on a two-unit property, you will prepare yourself mentally to turn down any single-family properties (unless they truly are a really great deal).

All of the methods presented here are used by investors every day to locate properties to buy. As you search for that first property, one thing will lead to another until you find a profitable deal. You cannot find that lucky, good deal unless you first invest time. You need to be out there looking every week and be prepared to act when it comes along.

Each of the real estate investors that I have met over the years have started out with small investments and built up their property portfolios as their experience and net worth grew. As you accumulate more properties, and the cash flow from them, your options as to the size of deals you can do and the methods of financing them increases.

Best ways to find bargains

You should consider having business cards printed that state, "I buy houses." Pass them out to everyone you meet, everywhere you go. Every now and then, a deal will come your way. It really does work. Read the classified ads every day, looking for bargains. Put signs up that say you buy houses. The main point is that you keep looking and you let everyone know you are looking. This is how you find the best deals.

Call the banks and savings and loan associations in your area and request a list of their foreclosures for sale.

Check with your County courthouse for information on tax sales; be sure you understand the auction rules.

Check the Internet for US Marshal sales of seized properties.

Drive residential streets looking for houses in safe areas in the poorest condition. Look up the owner in the courthouse records or online (county records) and send them a letter of inquiry, asking whether they would consider selling the house.

You can get a list of government property sales at www.pueblo.gsa.gov, a federal information center, by clicking on the Federal Programs – U.S.

Real Estate – Property Sales List page. This website lists government real estate properties sold by auction or sealed bid and explains how to get more information. The website also has a contact list of other dealers who auction government-seized property.

I met a husband-and-wife team a few years back who found homes for sale at bargain prices by looking at homes for rent in blue-collar neighborhoods every Thursday when the paper came out. They were seeking landlords who were disgruntled and fed up with being landlords. They would then offer to buy the house at a good price (good for them, that is). They had to look at hundreds of homes to find a deal, but it worked—they had seven when I met them. They knew the market; they offered a cash deal; and they closed on the deal within days. After closing, they took a mortgage out to replenish their funds. The plan was to offer $15,000 less than they thought the home was worth (condition being a consideration), and close the deal only if they could buy at $10,000 under market.

NAREI

Visit the website of the National Association of Real Estate Investors, www.narei.com, for local chapters in your area. Join the local chapter and let the other members know you are a buyer. There will be people there who scout deals and turn the deals over to investors for a fee. Expect to pay from $500 to $1500 to a scout who brings you a deal. There will also be people who buy fixer-uppers and sell them to investors.

Business cards

Print up 500 business cards that state, "I BUY HOUSES," with your name and contact information, including an e-mail address. Pass the cards out to everyone you meet and tell everyone that you are looking for houses to buy. Pass the cards out long enough and you'll inevitably find a good deal will come your way. You can also have signs printed and put them on roadsides that say, "I buy houses," with a phone number or e-mail address for people to reach you (check the local laws in your area on roadside signs).

Learn the market

Start looking at houses. Check the newspaper classifieds in your city for houses for sale. This is your new hobby at breakfast, at lunch, on break; you are reading the classified ads or reading a book about real estate. In order to know the values of homes and the current rental rates in different areas of town, you must look at a lot of houses. After looking at a hundred houses, you will know a bargain when you see it.

Look for words in the ads that might indicate a bargain, such as "for sale by owner," "handyman special," "rent-to-own," "low downpayment," etc. Call every ad. Do not become selective for the first two or three weeks. You are trying to learn all you can about the market and how different people handle the calls. If you start getting selective, you will miss a lot of opportunities and it will take longer to get comfortable with the process.

When you call, say, "I am calling about the house you have advertised. What you can tell me about it?" If they try to prequalify you, tell them you are looking for a home for your son or another relative and also for a rental property or two, preferably a duplex. That will get the person running the ad to provide you information without them having to nail you down on the details. Spend all your free time out looking at homes for sale or for rent.

"House for rent" ads

Check out the classified ads on houses for rent and pose as a potential tenant to see the properties. This will give you a feel for the rental rates in different parts of town. You will need such rental rate information to evaluate the cash flow of any potential purchase. As you look at rentals, you will meet all different types of landlords and learn the different ways that they operate. When you meet one that complains about being a landlord, you just may have found your bargain. This is how I found my first owner-financed house.

Houses in need of repair

When you are out looking at homes for sale and homes for rent, take note of any houses in need of repair or maintenance. Write down the property's address and search your city's tax records for the owner's address (most large cities have this information online), and send the owner a letter inquiring whether the house is for sale. There are a lot of absentee landlords that might sell if someone just asks. You might get told no a hundred times, but one yes can make you thousands of dollars.

Working with real estate agents

Real estate agents are working for the seller. It is their function to get the highest price for the property owners. Whenever possible, when buying, I prefer to deal directly with the sellers.[1] I have found that the downpayment required on properties when a real estate agent is involved is larger, even if the owner is financing the deal, because the seller's

---

[1] When selling to cash out, I usually use a real estate agent, as they are willing to help the buyer find financing.

closing costs typically run 8 to 10 percent of the house's sales price (with the agent's commission included).

Real estate agents, for the most part, are hardworking people and, if you are lucky enough to find a good one to work with, who brings you the kind of properties you are looking for, they can be a real boon. It would seem logical that real estate agents would recognize how real estate investors could increase their sales and commissions and would welcome a list of investors to work with who buy houses on a regular basis, however, oddly, I have not found that to be the case. So, rather than rely on real estate agents, proceed as if you must find every deal yourself. Then, when you are fortunate enough to find a good agent interested in helping you build a profitable inventory of rental properties, you will be ready to take advantage of that opportunity.

When selling a property with an owner-carried mortgage or contract for deed, I usually handle the sales and marketing myself. As I am providing the financing with a low downpayment, buyers are very easy to find and I can get a little more than appraised value with no commissions to pay.

Make the Deal

Prepare a cash budget

How much cash do you have to work with? Prepare a list of all your resources so that you know what you can and cannot do when you find a deal. You do not need to have any cash on hand, but you do need to know where you can get cash when you need it. List all the places that you can get cash: credit cards, credit union lines of credit, home equity credit lines, relatives, IRAs, savings, cash value of insurance policies, and possible investment partners. Try to increase your credit card limits wherever you can.

Do not take steps to borrow any money until and unless you have a deal—just keep $500 earnest money on hand. Money tends to disappear if you have it readily available. Borrowing money to make money is good business; borrowing money to spend is wasted interest expense.

What is a good deal?

The price of a property is not the sole criterion. The numbers have to work. By that I mean that the monthly rental cash income generated by the property must be sufficient to cover the mortgage payments, expenses, taxes, and insurance, and at least a little extra to provide a reasonable return on the cash invested.

As you are out looking at homes for sale, take notes. What is the asking price? How much are the taxes, insurance, utility and regular maintenance costs? Estimate any additional repair costs needed to get the house ready to rent.

With this information, you can determine how much monthly cash flow you would have if you purchased a particular property with different downpayments, different purchase prices, and rented at different rental rates. Do this exercise for the different parts of town and the different types of rentals, such as apartments, two-bedroom, and three-bedroom units. What you want to get a feel for, for instance, is what is the most you can pay for a three-bedroom house that produces a monthly gross rental income of, say, $750 and still have a positive cash flow.

When you find a property that will provide a positive cash flow with a downpayment you can afford, you have found a good deal. The rest of your profits will come from tax savings, equity buildup as the mortgage is paid down, appreciation, and any increase in value you add by sprucing up the place, as well as from future rent increases.

Making the deal

If you are doing the things outlined in this book, a deal *will* come along. When it does, do not talk it to death. Do not procrastinate. Do not play the "What if?" game until the deal goes to someone else. ACT! And act now. You have to just do it. Get that first deal under your belt. Get rid of the fear. As long as you crunch the numbers and they work, you'll be fine. Just do it!

Just do it!

The truth is, you have very little to lose and lots to gain. If you have been doing all I have suggested, you will be intimately familiar with the market, the rental rates, the bad areas of town (and even they can be good) and you have the numbers fairly well worked out. That makes the risk a calculated one, and that is the best you can expect. Even if you pay too much, time will fix it as the rental rates increase over time and the mortgage gets paid down. A negative cash flow will turn in to a positive cash flow.

The main thing is to make that first deal. Even if it does not do very well, it gets you started. I just about broke even on my first deal, selling it a year after I bought it. But I got started and that was the hardest part.

Buying Rental Houses

A word about taxes...

The business of rental property investing changed with the federal Tax Reform Act of 1986. Before the income tax law changed, you could use losses from rental properties to take your taxable earned income to zero. That allowed you a profit from tax savings, even if the property had a negative cash flow.

Today, you must plan on a positive cash flow because low inflation means that it can take years to get much appreciation in value. Of course, in some areas of the country, homes are increasing in price because of demand created by low interest rates. I would not count on low interest rates over the long term to create equity increases. Even with the changes to the tax laws, income-producing real estate is the best long-term investment for active investors.

Check the IRS pamphlets for passive loss rules and see www.irs.gov for all the latest updates regarding taxation of real estate investments. Remember, income from the real estate rental business is considered "passive" by the IRS.

Pursuant to IRS Publication 527 (2011), if you actively participate in the management, repairs, etc., of your rental property to the extent that you have passive income, you can offset that with any passive losses you may have from your rental business. If there are more losses than income to offset, you may then deduct the remaining losses from your other earned income.

Furthermore, there is a special allowance for rental losses. At the time of this writing, you can deduct up to $25,000 from your non-passive income. This deduction starts to phase out as your "modified" adjusted gross income (MAGI) exceeds $100,000. Then, the allowance is reduced by 50 percent of the amount over $100,000 and stops completely when you reach $150,000 MAGI. See IRS Publication 925 for more details. And, as always, when it comes to tax matters, because tax laws do change, be sure to consult your tax professional.

How rental real estate can make you money

The fastest method of increasing your net worth using rental real estate is to buy fixer-uppers and gain what's called sweat equity. Still, rental real estate offers multiple ways to make money on each deal. The rest of this book will outline them in a little more detail, and offer a few more ways to make money using real estate, plus some profit secrets. Some of these money-making options are:

1. Monthly positive cash flow from rental income

2. Income tax savings from depreciation

3. Equity increase by buying below market (appraised) value or by upgrading/making improvements

4. Protection from inflation by increasing rents over time

5. Appreciation/increase in the property's value over time

6. Equity buildup from paying down the principal mortgage balance via rental income

7. Interest income if you later sell the home and carry the mortgage note

8. Equity increase by raising rents and appraising the property based on net income

How much money do I need?

The dollars you need to make real estate investments range from zero up to 30 percent of the purchase price. That is the nice thing about single-family homes—they are everywhere, in all price ranges. The dollar amount of investment cash needed depends on where you get the money to finance the purchase.

If the homeowner is acting as their own sales agent and has a vacant property with payments due, they may let you buy it with no downpayment. Zero-down deals are hard to find and personally I do not like them because the seller has to bring a check with them to the closing to cover their costs.

If the mortgage money comes from a bank, the bank will want 20 to 30 percent down on rental homes. There are also homes with assumable notes, deals where the seller refinances the property to get some cash out and then sells it with owner financing. There are contracts for deed, notes, rent-to-own, bank repossessions, and many more methods to enable you to put a deal together. (For more on this, see "Financing" in chapter eight).

Which house to buy?

You should buy a house that will provide you with the most net monthly income (positive cash flow). The more net monthly income you end up with, the easier it will be to buy the next house. You also need a positive cash flow to do repairs, cover vacancies, and increase your net worth. The price of the home *by itself* is not important. What is more important is the net monthly rental income (after expenses),

Buy the house that generates the most cash

length of the tenant lease(s), condition of the home, estimated length of time to get it rented if vacant, the overall condition of that area of town, and the interest rate. You will find that each deal is different, and you must keep in mind your total monthly cost (in a ready-to-rent condition), and how that compares to the current rental income. If you cannot make the numbers work (yielding a positive net monthly income), it is not a deal.

What price to pay?

If the numbers do not work, any price is too high. By the time you make an offer on a home, I would hope that you would have looked at at least 50 houses to get a feel for the values, the neighborhoods, and the market's (current) rental rates. Do your homework because it will save you money and ideally make you money. A good deal is one where you end up with a net positive cash flow each month. Remember, you make your money when you buy right. You are not looking for the perfect deals, only the profitable deals.

What interest rate to accept?

This depends on the deal. A low interest rate with a large downpayment is not as good a deal as a higher interest rate with very small downpayment. Low interest rates combined with large downpayments means you will have a smaller interest deduction come tax time and, when you have a lot of cash tied up, you will not be able to do as many deals. Also, you will lose revenue on the large downpayment. A lower downpayment is better if everything else is good. You can always refinance if rates drop. I would rather have two homes where I paid $5,000 down on each (assuming positive cash flows) than one home where I paid $10,000 down.

Monthly expense total

You want, at minimum, expenses that total less than 80 percent of the monthly rental income on single-family houses. That would allow for a 20 percent vacancy factor while still permitting you to break even, such as if the house is vacant two months a year, and you would still have your tax savings and equity buildup from paying down the loan. Isn't that nice? Even if you break even in cash flow, you still get a little richer long term from increasing property values, future rent increases, and paying down the mortgage with the rent money.

Downpayment

The less money paid down the better. I try for four percent down. That is $1000 per $24,000 financed, with as low an interest rate as I can get. My favorite deal is one where the owner finances the house with $1000 down at six to 10 percent interest. I then refinance as soon as I have paid down the loan by 10 percent or more (which can take five-plus years).

I find the house, negotiate a deal with the seller, call the title company for an estimate of the closing costs for both the seller and me, and then I raise the downpayment enough so that the seller does not have to write a check at closing to sell the home, which helps keep the seller in a positive mood and they refrain from asking me to pay their costs at closing. I get to apply that amount to my equity position instead of covering their costs.

The seller will also be more inclined to cooperate when I ask for access to the house before closing to get it ready to rent the day after closing. That way, I collect a deposit and the first month's rent money from the renter weeks before my first mortgage payment is due. I set the mortgage up so that my first payment is not due for 45 days. I collect the second month's rent to cover my first payment. If I do this correctly, my cash flow covers my downpayment, or a large part of it.

Property condition

This depends on your investment style and your available cash. The closer the house is to being in a rentable condition, the better. The longer it takes to get a renter in the home, the more money you will need to float the deal. If the purchase price is low enough, I would take a fixer-upper and gain the sweat equity. Look at each deal on its own merits and consider your abilities and available time.

Location

If you want to charge a high rental rate to attract a better class of renter, you will want a property located in a good neighborhood with good schools. Otherwise, you will need a low-priced home that allows for cheaper rents to offset a less than desirable location. The longer someone stays in your house, the better.

People will stay in a home year after year for lots of reasons. One of the primary reasons is because their kids are in school. If the area and the schools are not the best, you will need cheaper rents than are available elsewhere in town.

Buy rental properties in the city where you live, as you will be more familiar with the area and management will be easier.

Finance terms

If cash flow or resale in the near future is your goal, then 30-year mortgages, preferably with assumable loans, are best. If you plan to hold the home until it is paid for and then sell the house and carry back the mortgage yourself, then a 20-year mortgage will pay the home off faster. Avoid balloon notes of any kind (notes where a lump sum comes due), unless you are an experienced investor and have the assets to get a loan under whatever conditions may be prevailing at the time the lump sum comes due. The longer the term, the lower the payment, and the larger the net cash flow. The shorter the term of the loan, the faster equity builds up as the mortgage is paid down, and the lower your net cash flow will be. (For more on this, see "Where The Real Estate Profits Are" later on in this chapter.)

Multi-family homes

Multi-family homes are better than single-family homes because they produce more cash flow, but they are harder to sell, as most buyers prefer single-family homes. Look for duplexes or homes with garage apartments, or even small apartment buildings. Be very careful when considering large homes that have been converted into apartments as they are often poorly converted, lack sufficient parking, and are very hard to sell later.

Unless you get into buying large apartment complexes, you will find that what applies to buying and renting single-family homes also applies to multi-family. The biggest advantage to multi-family properties is that more than one renter on a property can improve the cash flow and lower your vacancy risk. Check for adequate parking space when buying multiple dwelling units on the same property. Parking problems are the number one complaint of tenants.

When and Where to Buy Rental Real Estate

When to buy

The timing has to do with location and events. Real estate sales and values run in cycles and different types of real estate have different cycles. For example, the number of real estate sales and the prices paid for that real estate would both be higher in the direction a city is growing. Sales and prices may also improve when a large employer moves into an area.

85

Many events affect the interest in a particular area and/or type of real estate, such as tax rates, city growth, highway construction, interest rates, employer relocation, university expansion, etc.

Your job is to educate yourself on real estate investing and getting your financial house in order so you can take advantage of opportunity when it arrives. You do this by reading the local paper, driving around with your eyes open, and asking yourself, "How can I profit from this event?"

After you have done this a few times, an idea will pop into your head, which you should investigate as an exercise in possibilities. What you want to accomplish by doing this is to change your way of thinking about what it is you see, read, and hear. You want to view the world through the lens of an investor, to learn to think like an investor.

Next, we will discuss some of the events that affect real estate and what you might target. Timing your purchases to take place just before prices are about to go up is a function of your local real estate knowledge, experience, and willingness to act on that gut feeling.

When interest rates are low

Home sales go up, and so do the prices, when interest rates are low. It is a good time to buy a home to live in, but not to rent, unless you plan to hold the property for a long time. The exception is when the low interest rates last for years and older homes begin to sit on the market a long time. You can, with due effort, find a seller who has two

It's sometimes best to buy when rates are high

mortgage payments and must sell, thus getting a bargain price.

The way to decide whether to buy a house you are considering as a rentable property is to determine the annual rental income, minus your annual cost of owning the property (taxes, insurance, utilities, and maintenance). If you are willing to live with that amount of cash flow for a long time, say 10 years, then go ahead and buy the property.

When interest rates are low, it is a good time to look into buying apartment buildings because, after several years of low interest rates, apartment building vacancies rise due to occupants buying homes, and the value of any apartment building is based upon vacancy rate and rental income. Empty apartments and low rents mean less value and, therefore, lower purchase prices, and low interest rates means lower payments for you, the buyer. You know when the timing is right to buy when you see move-in incentives being offered at apartment buildings. It is time to start looking.

If you are a developer of a new property, low interest rates will reduce the carrying costs of a project and make some projects doable that might not be advisable during periods with higher interest rates.

The higher the interest rate, the better—why is that?

High interest rates mean it is a good time to be a rental house investor/ buyer because homebuyers do not buy when rates are high and new home construction comes to a standstill, plus, there are more potential tenants looking to rent instead. You have little or no home-buying competition in the market. If sellers cannot sell their homes on the open market, they will have to sell to you and carry the mortgage themselves.

Look for older homes where the current owner has no mortgage. You offer to buy at 10 percent below the market value with a small downpayment and owner financing at seven to 10 percent interest or less.

If interest rates come down in a few years, you can sell the home, refinance it, or raise the rent every year until the place is paid for. I would look for duplexes or homes with garage apartments for the dual income.

City growth plans

Major cities have growth plans and you should check with your City Hall to learn more. Check the city's growth wish list and try to determine what area is in development or what part of the plan is likely to become a reality. Start looking in the area(s) where the city is most likely to expand.

In San Antonio, for example, Austin Highway has a redevelopment committee that has been working for years to attract new businesses. Those people who purchased property early on have made out very well, as there is now a lot of new construction going on.

When new homes are selling well

When interest rates are low, there is a high rate of new home sales. In this situation, I look in the older neighborhoods for fixer-upper homes. The demand for fixer-uppers will be lower when new homes are selling well, as most people prefer a new home or at least one that needs no work, so you can sometimes find bargains because there is much less competition.

Older areas of town

Do not ignore the older areas of town. If all the growth is heading in one direction, check out the other areas of town for opportunity. While everyone is focused on that high growth area, what is being ignored in other areas? What real estate is needed there?

Is there a need for apartments, car lots, or strip centers, for instance? Are there areas where the homeowners are beginning to make improvements to their homes? Can you buy the worst home on the block and fix it up?

Are there strip shopping centers that need sprucing up? Buildings that need converting? Is there a need for a self-storage facility?

Future highway development plans

Check with your nearest state highway department and review the five- and 10-year highway construction plans. This is especially important when purchasing or leasing commercial properties. The changing of, or improvements to, a street or highway can dramatically affect a property's value.

For example, if a highway's off ramp is going to be moved back so that a property is now situated following the off ramp instead of behind it, it stands to gain more value in a buyer's eyes. Streets that undergo improvements will increase property values if new amenities are added, such as sidewalks, curbs and lighting. A commercial property's value and its rental value rise after new street improvements have been completed but the tenants can go broke during an extended construction period.

Other events

Other real estate development can and will drive demand for surrounding real estate. A new Wal-Mart will increase the value of surrounding land because of increased traffic flow. A new, large manufacturing plant will create demand for apartments, warehouses, retail store space, car lots, cafes, and homes. Be aware of the events and happenings in your chosen trade area and be prepared to invest when the deal is right for you. Keep in mind that you only need three or four good deals in a lifetime to be well off.

Train Yourself to Spot Opportunities

Train your mind to view problems and obstacles as opportunities. Ask yourself, "How can I use this to my advantage?" There are so few people doing this that you will have a distinct advantage. How do you train yourself to think this way? Every time someone mentions a problem of any kind, on any subject, not just your investment interest, ask yourself: "What is the opposite? What are the positives?" People are always talking about problems at work, in their personal relationships, at school, everywhere. Any time someone mentions a problem, think of what the positive outcomes could be? Ask the "What if?" questions.

View obstacles as opportunities

Practice looking for the positive aspects of any and every problem until it becomes a habit. While everyone else is dwelling on the negatives, you dwell on the positives, the possibilities, and a funny thing will happen—people will want to be around you more. You will begin to gain a reputation as a smart person. Your advice will become sought after.

There are two types of people who attract others, like bees to honey. Those are people with positive outlooks and attitudes, and people with bubbly personalities. Become one of the two or both. Add to that increased knowledge of how to make money and you will be well on your way along the road to riches.

EXAMPLE

A friend of mine was looking at a 40-unit apartment building. The real estate agent said the seller was anxious to sell, but, when pressed, gave vague reasons. My friend returned to the property after the agent had left and spoke to the manager. Tenant turnover was high, he discovered, as tenants seldom renewed their leases, and the manager said it was because of the resident children making too much noise, young people playing loud music, and the poor condition of the laundry equipment. The current owner's solution was to offer discounts for longer-term leases.

Due to the high vacancy factor and the low income from discounted rents, my friend purchased the building at a good price. He immediately purchased new laundry machines, changed the name of the apartments, and added below the name on the sign, "Retirement Apartments – Age 55 and Older." As leases expired, he declined to renew and, instead, rented only to those aged 55 and older. Eventually, the tenant problems were resolved and he got a bit richer.

Mobile homes

Considering the economy and the reluctance of banks to lend money to investors, it's helpful to know your options for making money in real estate with more modest investments.

Over the last few decades I have bought and sold a few mobile homes. Further, I have met several men who have and do make tens of thousands of dollars from owning mobile homes. One man I know in Texas has 22 rental units. His rental income is in excess of $12,000 per month.

Another man I know there owns a mobile home park. Whenever anyone left and relocated their mobile home, he populated the lot with used mobile homes. He had previously gotten $225–295 rent per month for the lot; by providing the used mobile homes as well, he began renting at an average of $650 per month instead. The used mobile homes cost $5000–10,000 each, giving him a 100 percent or more return on his initial investment in one to two years.

Renting is not the only way to make money with used mobile homes. You can also buy, fix up, and sell them, sell them on a rent-to-own basis, buy them for cash and then sell them on an owner-carried note and make 20 percent plus annual returns on your money, or you could do a combination of any or all of these.

Let's look at each of these possibilities and run some numbers.

Renting mobile homes can be very profitable and a low-cost way of getting into the rental housing business. Suppose you buy a used two-bedroom mobile home for $8000, for which you pay rent on the lot, and spend $2000 sprucing it up, for a total investment of $10,000. You rent this unit for $650 a month. Your lot rent will likely range about $250–300 a month, leaving you with $350 a month cash flow. After taxes, your cash flow should be about $3500 a year. That is a payback, a full 100 percent return on your investment, of 28 months—in less than three years you have all your money back. Get ten of these and you have a real nice extra income. I prefer the singlewide units because doublewide units cost more to buy and set up, yet the rent is not that much higher.

Buying and selling mobile homes can be a nice profitable sideline, too, and/or a way to pay for rentals. Using the same example, you buy a singlewide mobile home for $8000. You spend $3000 to $5,000 fixing it up to sell. That will mean just slightly nicer upgrades and fixtures than for a rental. You want the customer to say, "Wow!" when they walk in the door. New decorator paint, new carpet, new bathroom fixtures, new faucets and lighting, etc. And you stage the home like a model home. You list the unit for sale at $25,000. Your classified ad might look like this:

For sale: newly remodeled mobile home,

14' x 56' 2/1[2] like new; easy qualifying;

$25,000 owner-financed, $2000 down
$667/mo. incl. lot rent

---

[2] Two bedrooms and one bath.

You sell the home somewhere between $22,000 and $25,000 with $2000 down, and finance the buyer at 14 percent interest. If you carry the note for $20,000 at 14 percent for six years, their payment is $412 a month. If you carry 18,000 at 14 percent for six years, their payment is $371 per month. They will pay because they can't live anywhere else more cheaply than that. You then either sell the note or use it to borrow at the bank for your next deal. There are plenty of people who will buy 14 percent notes.

Alternatively, you could do both. You could sell a few and use those profits to finance your rental fleet until you have enough rental units to provide the monthly cash flow sufficient for your needs.

EXAMPLE

I purchased a singlewide mobile home in 2009 from a woman who was clearing her mother's estate. She asked $10,000 and told me she had only received offers less than $6,000. So, I offered her a choice of $6000 cash or $8000 with $1000 down and $1000 per month for seven months at zero interest. She jumped on that last deal. I estimated I would need to spend $5000–10,000 on remodeling to get the trailer into a respectable "for sale" condition home. I was looking for the "Wow!" factor to enable me to get the highest price possible from my investment. The mobile home park ($300 lot rent) did not allow rentals, so a sale was my only option. The home was on a corner lot with a huge oak tree in the front yard so I knew it would show well.

The living room needed new paint, trim, carpet, ceiling fan, switch and plug covers and smoke detector. The dinette area needed new paint, trim and ceiling light. The kitchen needed new paint, touching up cabinet stains, new flooring, new lights, stove escutcheons, and a good cleaning. The bedrooms both got new carpet, paint, trim and light fixtures, and the bathroom/laundry needed new flooring, new shower pan, new shower surround, new plumbing and showerhead, new toilet, new vanity and

93

mirror, new towel cabinet, new light, new trim, new smoke detector and the water heater repaired.

I also replaced the exterior light fixtures, installed shutters, added to and repaired the fence, repainted the rear stoop, rebuilt the front landing, and trimmed the trees and landscaping. Total purchase and upgrade: $18,000.

I sold it for $25,000.

The numbers

The cost to buy the trailer, remodel it and pay the lot rent during the three-month holding period was $18,900. I financed the buyer with $2000 down at 14 percent interest for ten years.

Amount financed to buyer	$23,000
Monthly principal and interest	$357
Total interest income over 10 years	$19,854
Total principal and interest paid to me	$42,854

How hard was it to sell? I sold the house in ten days from a classified ad I ran in the Thrifty Nickel classifieds to the second person who looked at the unit. She was a single mother with two children. It was easy to sell because I was financing it, and the monthly payments were comparable to renting an apartment. The buyer got a "like new" home to own for the same amount as rent. That, dear investor, was an easy sale.

What if they don't keep up the payments? Remember, the primary incentive is that there is nowhere they can live for less. So, check their credit, their job history, and, if they fail to pay, repossess, touch up, and resell.

Where the Real Estate Profits Are

Throughout this book, we discuss methods and ideas that you can use to make money from your real estate investments. Some of the ideas and methods in this section are a clarification of areas already discussed, and some are new. As you open up your mind to the many ways an income-producing property can make you money, you will begin to see opportunity where you only saw problems before.

You will have found your road to wealth.

Profit first when you buy it

Negotiate! *You make your first profit when you buy a property.* Every dollar you pay under the market price for a property is net worth to you on your financial statement. Buy based on the property's current economic value or the property's current "as is" value. Then you can improve the net operating income and/or the property's condition to improve the overall value.

> **Every dollar you pay under market adds a dollar to your net worth**

Make your offer subject to someone inspecting the property or to satisfactory remodeling estimates, etc. What you are looking for is a reason to renegotiate the price after the deal is accepted, just in case you discover something later that needs fixing. On a commercial deal this is called due diligence, but in residential contracts in some areas you may need to add that clause.

The clause I use is: *"This contract is subject to the buyer receiving an acceptable repair estimate from [repair company name]."*[3] This clause lets you tie up the property and renegotiate the price if the cost comes in higher than anticipated.

Key point

Every dollar you save at the time of purchase is worth three times that amount if you consider interest paid over thirty years. You make your first profit when you make the purchase. This is also the time to get the terms that will allow you the most future flexibility.

Sweat equity

Always get your repair estimates from a general contractor. You negotiate the purchase price based on having a contractor do the repairs and then, if you subcontract the repairs or do them yourself, you pocket the profit the contractor would have made. (See "Home Improvements that Pay" in chapter eleven for more information.)

Interest rate profits

There are several ways to make or save money on interest rates.

1. Negotiate and shop around. The Internet makes this easy to do.

---

[3] I have a friend's name I fill in who operates as a liaison so that I am not tied to a specific contractor or individual.

2. When you are quoted a rate, ask for a lower one. The institution may come back with a lower offer with different terms. Half the time, I negotiate a slightly better deal.

3. Assume any previously existing loans possible that are at low rates.

4. If the owner is financing the deal, offer a rate that is two or three points over bank CD rates, which are usually lower than mortgage rates.

5. As a buyer, avoid due on sale or prepayment penalty clauses, as this will give you a chance to sell the house by offering financing and wrapping your existing mortgage with one at a higher interest rate than you are paying and you can make the interest spread. (In other words, you make money on the difference in the interest rates between the note you are paying and the one being paid to you.) This is easier to do with owner financing.

6. Refinance if rates drop two or more percentage points. This is your chance to get cash out, lower your payment, or shorten your loan term. Check the total cost first.

Cash flow

If you buy right, you should have a positive cash flow each month on your purchases.

Cash flow is determined by calculating all the rental income and subtracting expenses, such as the cost of maintenance, taxes, insurance, utilities, and the principal and interest payments.

EXAMPLE

Let's say you have a two-unit duplex, rented at $500 per unit per month. The total cost was $100,000 with $10,000 down and a mortgage of $90,000 at seven percent for 30 years.

Your gross income the first year is $500 x 2 units x 12 months = $12,000.

Your costs that year are $1,250 taxes, $400 insurance, $250 repairs, and $200 miscellaneous, for a total of $2100. But, you also have to figure in the interest on the mortgage: $90,000 at seven percent, which equals $6300 (excluding any principal payment). So, $2100 operating expense plus $6300 interest means your total costs for the first year come to $8400.

$12,000 gross income – $8400 total costs = $3600 annual profit.

If your mortgage payments are $599 per month, then the first year would cost you $7188. If you subtract the annual interest payment of $6300, you are left with an annual principal paydown of $888.

Now subtract the $888 from the profit of $3600 and you have a **positive cash flow** of $2212.

The overall return on the downpayment invested was 36 percent. The return on the cash downpayment, not including the principal payment, is 22 percent.

Wraparound mortgage magic

A wraparound mortgage, often referred to simply as a wrap, is a mortgage that is essentially "wrapped" around a previously existing one. Envision a property you purchased, financed with a mortgage that does not have to be paid off in full when you sell. When you do sell the property, you offer seller financing to your buyer at a higher interest rate than you are paying, or for a longer term, or both. Instead of paying off your own mortgage, you increase your monthly cash flow by taking the mortgage payment from your buyer each month and applying it to your less expensive underlying mortgage, pocketing the difference. I do this with a contract for deed until my underlying mortgage is paid off.

There are some creative things being done with wraparound mortgages. Here is one way to use them to make money. You buy a house at a good price with owner financing and no due on sale clause. You spruce it up. Then you sell the house for a higher price with a low downpayment at a higher interest rate than you are paying.

EXAMPLE

You buy an owner-financed house for $40,000 at seven percent for 20 years. After a little sprucing up, you sell the house for $48,000 with a small downpayment and you owner-finance the house at 12 percent for 30 years. You make money several ways.

- The equity increase from the price increase

- The buyer's longer finance term (30 vs. 20 years) means more of each payment you receive will consist of interest (i.e., pure profit for you)

- The longer-term note will pay you a further 10 years after your underlying note has been paid off

- The higher interest rate you charge (vs. what you pay) allows you a profit from the interest rate spread

This example assumes that the downpayments cancel each other out and that you can cover the sprucing up cost out of your own pocket. Also, if your buyer pays you off early, some of your gains will go away. You can delay that time by inserting into the contract a penalty clause for early payoff during the first five years.

These deals are done every day and you can do them, too. There are buyers out there who would not qualify for a conventional mortgage who would love for you to do a deal like this. There are sellers who want a quick sale without repairs who will carry your note if you are buying.

Key point

If you want to do these deals, you must always look out for them, and you lay the groundwork when you buy the house by leaving your options open. As a buyer, you must *avoid* a due on sale clause. You want a 20-year mortgage and a low interest rate. You lock in the profits when you sell by *including* a due on sale clause in the contract *you* offer, charging a higher interest rate than you are paying, and selling with a 30-year mortgage, including an early payoff penalty.

Equity buildup

This is my favorite way that real estate makes you money. Every time you buy a property and rent it out, you create a cash flow to cover the mortgage payments. You pay for your property with other people's money, thus making yourself a little richer every month. That is a very powerful statement. And no income tax is due on this mortgage reduction until you sell the property, if then. The more rental properties you have, the richer you get each month. *Think about it!*

The problem the average person has when trying to get rich is that they only have 24 hours a day in which they can sell their services to make money. In order to get rich, you have to solve this problem. One way to do that is to start a company and hire people to work for you. Hopefully, you can make a profit on their labors. It works, but has a high failure rate. Another way to solve the problem is to buy rental properties on credit and pay the loans off with other people's labor paid to you in the form of monthly rent. That is a much less risky way of getting rich.

Taxes

The tax law changes that occurred in 1986 and again in 2004 had a substantial effect on real estate investing, mainly because one can no longer shelter all of one's earned income[4] from taxes by taking real estate losses.[5]

You can still shelter some of your earned income using the income tax deduction from the interest paid on mortgages, property repair expenses, and the operating expenses, all of which are deductible against the property's income at tax time. The buildings and improvements to them may be depreciated to further reduce your income tax liability. The mileage you drive to find the properties or to visit the properties after you buy provides a nice tax deduction. The profit from increasing prices and equity buildup are taxable only when you sell the property, and may not be taxable even then. You can exchange the property rather than sell it to delay the taxes even longer and, if you pass the properties on to your estate, the taxes may never have to be paid.

I do recommend that you visit www.irs.gov and read their bulletins on real estate and tax laws.

---

[4] If you make over $100,000 per year, see your accountant as you may not be able to take full advantage of real estate investment tax savings.

[5] See IRC§ 469

Property value appreciation bonus

This is where the bonus money comes from. Many things can affect the value of real estate, such as schools, neighborhood, crime rates, street improvements, inflation, a new development nearby, etc.

Let us assume you buy a house and, two years later, the city repaves your street, puts in new sidewalks and curbs, and you get a new driveway entrance at little or no cost to you. The elementary school builds a new building. A new grocery store and movie theater open up less than a mile away. Inflation is only two percent per year, yet your house goes up 12 percent in value because of all these other positive events that make your location more desirable. You do not get this money until you sell, but you can get a form of it when the leases expire and you raise the rent or refinance the house to take out cash. The more homes you own, the more the chances you have to reap these extra bonuses.

EXAMPLE

A friend of mine had a piece of commercial property he was thinking of selling for about $250,000. He put up a sign that said "Available – 1 acre, Sale/Lease/Build to Suit." He priced it at $275,000, leaving a little room to negotiate. Instead of selling the property, which would create a tax liability, he leased it, giving the lessee an option to buy any time during the following five years for $300,000.

By not selling the property, my friend got $50,000 richer than he had been before leasing it. What did the lease accomplish? He had a monthly income to cover the note he owed the bank. The lessee was now paying the taxes and maintenance costs.

Not having actually sold the property, my friend did not owe capital gains taxes, thus all of the equity was still at work for him. He got a higher potential sales price than an outright sale would have produced, thus getting $50,000 richer. He saved the real estate sales commission as the lessee has the option to buy at a set price with no agent required. The property value increased because the value is now the economic value of the lease rather than the area's property value comparisons.

He can borrow money if need be, based on the property's new economic value, backed up by the lease. The bank will be more inclined to make a loan, taking the property as collateral, because the property's value has been declared. The lease can be assigned to the bank and the owner has income from the property to pay back the loan in addition to his guarantee. The bank will have three ways in which to get repaid, all of which makes the loan more secure.

The lessee gets to control the property's use without a large downpayment, and has a set purchase price that won't increase. The purchase option also protects the value of the lessee's property improvements. Because the lessee plans on improving the property, when he is ready to buy he will have the equity needed to get the bank loan, as the improvements will increase the appraised value of the property compared to the fixed price of his purchase option. This is a win-win deal.

Improvement profits

You can make money on some improvements. You must, however, do your homework and be certain that the cost of the improvement will be offset by higher rents and improved value.

The two questions to ask yourself are:

- Will the next buyer be willing to pay as much, or more, than I paid for this improvement?

and

- Will the tenant pay more per month if I make this improvement?

A few weeks ago, I visited my daughter at her new apartment. The apartment complex had detached garages and storage rooms. When I commented on them, she informed me that the garages were $50 extra per month, and the storage rooms were $25 extra.

What could you do to improve your property and/or increase the income? Carports? Storage? Convert a garage to an apartment? Add an apartment over the garage? *Think!*

Rent increases

You profit from rent increases two ways. First, your cash flow improves, and, second, the higher the property's net income, the more an investor will pay for the property when you sell it. Every six months, you should check the rental rates on properties similar to yours and increase the rents as needed. When you are buying, you want to find landlords who have not kept up with the market rents, and, when you are selling, you want to sell based on the highest possible market rents.

Highest and best uses

Once you own a property, you should consider if a change in the property's use would increase the income and, thus, the value. Some properties are already operating at their highest and best use, and there is no alternative use that would increase their potential value. Others will have that potential. You should review any properties you own to see if there is a better, more profitable use. A few of these ideas are furnished below to get your imagination started.

- Adding a garage apt

- Converting a single-family into a duplex

- Changing the zoning

- Changing the tenant type

- Converting from month-to-month rentals to leases

- Adding another building on the same land

Real Estate Profit Secrets

Here we will cover the ideas, techniques, and/or methods that I have used or heard of in order to make a few extra dollars on a deal. For those of you who have been at real estate investing for a while, this may not be new. But, if one idea saves or makes you money, we will have succeeded.

Keep in mind that, with real estate investing, your dollars can be leveraged three or four times. For every dollar you have to invest, you can borrow three more dollars (at a minimum) to put to work. If you have $10,000 to invest, then you can borrow $30–40,000 more.

The investment money you use to leverage a loan can be in the form of equity rather than cash. As the values of the properties you buy improve, because you have improved the properties or rental income, you can use that increased equity to borrow even more. That is the magic of real estate investing. A little money combined with leverage, time, good management, and experience equals wealth.

Ownership

For most investors, holding property as individuals is the best method because the tax advantages and cash flow will then pass through to you. Holding title in your name does, however, expose you to unlimited liability, so be sure to carry a high dollar, blanket-type liability insurance policy. I carry a general million-dollar policy plus million-dollar policies on each property I own. The cost is relatively low.

Any real estate you use in your business should be owned by you personally and leased back to your business. By holding title to business property in your name, you will be able to take maximum advantage of the tax laws. The only exception I can think of is when the property stores hazardous chemicals.

Vacancy can be good

Check the rental market rates at least once a year, and even more often in good economic times. As a rule, property values are about 100 times the net monthly rental income. If you raise the rent by $25 per month, you increase the value of the building by $2,500. There are thousands of properties out there that would have a better rate of return, and thus a higher resale value, if the rents were set at the going market rates.

You can buy a building at its current economic value and raise the rent to make it more profitable, and thus more valuable. If you look at a building that is 100 percent occupied, chances are the rental rates are too low.

Similar types of apartment tenants

If you own an apartment building, think about renting your apartments to a certain type of tenant, e.g., over 55s, single adults, or students. It makes advertising easier, and people will pay a little bit more to live with a group in which they feel comfortable. Each group has its advantages. For example, retired couples like to live with others in that "over 55" age group. There is less tenant turnover and they tend to be better credit risks with less wear and tear to the units.

Mortgage length

Check the difference in monthly payments on 15-, 20-, and 30-year mortgages. The interest savings can be very substantial if you plan on holding the property until maturity.

EXAMPLE

A mortgage of $80,000 at seven percent for 30 years has a principal and interest payment of $532. At 20 years, the payment is $620, and, at 15 years, the payment is $719.

Carefully consider payment amount and interest paid over time against your investment objectives. If you are managing with an eye to the monthly cash flow, so that you can own as many houses as possible, then take the lowest payment. If building up equity is more important than cash flow, take the higher payment. The longer the term, the lower the payment amount and the bigger the interest tax deduction. Remember, you can always pay down more per month on the principal to reduce the number of years until maturity.

Assumable loans

When buying a house, try to assume any outstanding loans if they are at lower than current interest rates. Before you agree to pay off an old loan, do the math to see if assuming the old loan and taking a second for the balance would be cheaper than a new mortgage for the entire amount. A lot of old, assumable loans have no due on sale clauses and they might save you from having to pay points on a new loan. (These are getting harder to find.)

Avoiding ARMs

Adjustable rate mortgages (ARMs) start out with a low "teaser" interest rate and increase substantially over just a few years if interest rates rise, upping your monthly payments. Should you consider adjustable rate mortgages? Rule of thumb: If you plan to sell the property or refinance it within five years, go for the lower rate ARM; if you are planning on holding the property for six or more years, take a fixed-rate loan.

The reason has to do with the way interest rates increase and the math. Interest rates go up and down slowly, generally over about a two- or three-year period. If a low variable interest rate holds for two years and then starts to climb slowly and steadily for two or more years, you will be dollars ahead or, at worst, break even for the first five years with the ARM. After five years of increasing interest rates, the fixed rates will have become more economical.

Negotiating real estate sales commissions

That's right. *Real estate sales commissions are negotiable.* Ask for a lower commission rate if the agent is asking you to lower your selling price or pay points to a bank on behalf of the buyer. Just keep in mind that all parties to a real estate deal are making money, or hope to. *Everything is negotiable*, including the sales commission.

Some agents will take a note for their commission, or part of it. They do not like it but, once in a while, it can help close the money gap and save a deal. This works best with independent agents who are acting as both the listing and selling broker.

If a property's sales price is over $300,000 you should pay less than the so-called "standard" 6 percent commission—4 to 4.5 percent is plenty. On deals over a million dollars, 2 or 3 percent is usually fair. If you are in a seller's market and you want to get top dollar for your home, try a commission plan designed to give the agents an incentive to sell at a higher price.

Let's say your agent wants to list your home for $350,000 with a 6 percent commission and they think it will bring between $320,000 and $350,000. Consider setting the commission at 4 percent of the first $300,000 and 15 percent of any amount over the $300,000. If the home sells for $320,000, you pay commission of $15,000. If it sells for $350,000, you pay commission of $19,500, 5.6 percent of the sales price. The difference is that you net more from the sale, and the agent has the incentive to negotiate the higher sales price.

Do not pay any extra fees to the agency listing your property for sale. The sales commission is more than adequate. Keep your listings to three months at a time. Six months is entirely much too long for residential properties, and long listings encourage real estate agents to procrastinate.

If the agencies insist on the longer listing, you need to insist on a month-by-month marketing plan specific to your property. Most listing contracts have a clause that states you must pay a commission to the agent if a buyer the agent brings around buys the home after a listing expires. Be very certain that you insert a clause that states that this pay-later clause does not apply if you have the home later listed for sale with any other agency. You do not want to find out later that you owe two commissions.

Offsetting downpayment cash with rental income

On a multi-tenant building, if you close the deal just after the first of the month, the rent credit and deposit credits that you get will offset part of your downpayment and your closing costs. Set your closing date for the third day of the month, just after the rents are collected, to maximize the current cash received. When buying a property, I set my closing for the fifth day of the month in order to get the maximum cash from the existing rentals an entire month before my mortgage payment is due.

Trading properties to postpone taxes

The downpayment need not be cash. Consider trading services or equity in other property for the downpayment. If you are planning to sell one property to buy another, a trade could postpone any income tax due (see irs.gov for current real estate tax law information). Check with your accountant to be sure the deal is structured correctly to meet the IRS's like-kind exchange rules, thus postponing the capital gains tax you would pay on a sale.

Depreciation

Whenever you cannot write something off as repairs on your rental properties, such as replacing all of the refrigerators in the complex, make sure to get a letter or other proof from the supplier or manufacturer showing the useful life expectancy of the item(s). It may be that you can depreciate those items over a shorter period of time than the standard depreciation schedule (SDS) of 27.5 years. For instance, you might be able to depreciate the refrigerators over a 10-year lifespan instead.

The rules for depreciation with regard to rental property can be confusing. For instance, things like sinks, outlets, paint, pipes, lights and electrical wiring, are all considered structural components of the building and must be depreciated over the 27.5 year SDS.[6] Make sure you check with your tax professional. Don't forget: educate yourself as much as you can. The tax codes are online and the law library in your local courthouse is free.

Owner-financing magic

When buying a property, I will pay more to obtain owner financing (more interest and/or a higher price) as long as I can write the contract. You want to buy and finance the deal without a due on sale clause, and you want to get an assumable mortgage. This gives you greater flexibility when you sell the house, and the possibility of getting a discount when you do offer to pay off the mortgage in the future.

EXAMPLE

You buy a house with an owner-carried note. A few years later, you decide to sell the house and your buyer is getting a new VA loan, which will pay *your* loan off. You call up your note holder and offer to pay them off in the next 30 to 60 days if they will discount the note. Ask for a $1,000 discount or two percent off the balance. You will be surprised by how many times they will take you up on your offer. When they do say yes, type up a letter to that effect, get it signed

---

[6] Reyes, Carrie B. "Component depreciation barred by standard depreciation schedule." *first tuesday journal online.* 25 May 2012.

right away, and take it to the title company. The letter will become part of the closing instructions.

When your existing loan is at a low interest rate and the rates have increased, even banks will say yes to a discounted early payoff as they can then loan that money at a higher rate.

Or, if your mortgage note does not have a due on sale clause, you can sell the house on a wraparound mortgage where your buyer pays you monthly and you continue to pay your old note (which is at a lower interest rate and for a shorter time period). You then get to pocket the difference each month. However, you can only do the wraparound mortgage if you do not have a due on sale clause in your original mortgage.

Escrow payments

I personally do not keep escrow accounts. If you have the discipline to save the money so that you will have the money when the taxes and insurance payments come due, then why tie up your money (interest free) in escrow accounts when you could put that money to work?

Real Estate Buying Tips and Ideas

- When buying investment properties, take your time. Check to see if it will be a profitable deal. Do not buy the property because you like it; buy only if it will yield a positive return.

- Most real estate agents are not familiar with how to analyze an income-producing property. Even if they are, you should be prepared to do the analysis yourself or use an accountant familiar with income-producing real estate.

- When using equity from one property to buy another (equity then becomes cash invested), be sure the return on the funds used is a reasonable one, say, 10 percent or more. I try for 20 percent-plus. This

If it doesn't make money, why do it?

means the net profit on the new property needs to make you a fairly safe 10 percent-plus on your cash invested.

- In my opinion, seller financing is always the best, and I'll tell you why: *the loans do not show up on your credit report.* A seller can finance all or part of the deal and earn a higher rate from you than a CD pays. If the seller finances the deal, you can set any terms you both agree to. Seller financing gives you the most flexibility to structure a deal.

- Rule of thumb for a good deal: The price you pay should be no more than 70 to 80 percent of the value of the property. The total cost of the property *after all repairs are done* should not exceed 80 percent of the property's appraised value. You can fudge this a little if you are pleased with the net monthly cash flow. This means that, when you look at a property, you calculate the property's value after it is put in first-class order and offer a price that is only about 75 percent of that value, including the cost of getting the property to that first-class condition.

- Locate properties with out-of-town owners (i.e., landlords), and send them letters offering to buy their property; they may be more motivated to sell.

- If a home on a block is a little worn around the edges compared to the surrounding homes, it may be a rental. Try to find the owner and see if a deal can be made.

- If there are any new banks in your town, they may be hungry for business and offer you better rates.

- You may be able to depreciate certain improvements to your rental property over a shorter period than the IRS depreciation tables, depending on their projected lifespan. You will need evidence of the useful life of the item from the supplier or manufacturer. Check with your tax professional as to what items can be depreciated on this shorter schedule.

- Buy when rental rates and interest rates are low—your profits will only increase as rates go up.

- No-money-down real estate deals are attractive *only if the deal has a positive monthly cash flow after payments and expenses are considered.* In other words, if you are not going to make money, why do it at all?

- Have an exit plan every time you make a purchase of real estate. Are you going to rent it? Fix it up and cash out? Trade up to another property? Your exit strategy will affect how you value the property.

- Join a real estate investors club, if one is available in your area. These can provide you with great contacts and opportunities for learning.

- Tie up the property you are considering with a small deposit while you check out the possibilities. You do not want to check out repair costs, values, zoning possibilities, rental rates, etc., only to have someone more nimble buy the property out from under you.

- If you are buying fixer-uppers to build your wealth, do not overpay. I wouldn't pay more than 60 to 70 percent of the post-repair value myself. If you underestimate repairs you will need the margin.

- Read the real estate section of the newspaper every Sunday—know what is happening in your town. I would suggest you read the business paper, also.

- A good credit rating will save you tens of thousands of dollars in lower interest rate charges over a lifetime. Protect your credit. It is your best asset.

- Set up a reserve to cover any unforeseen expenses or vacancies. I recommend 10 to 33 percent of monthly net cash flow (I use 33 percent). This fund covers vacancies, emergency repairs, and tax bills. Without it, I could well have fallen behind on my payments during tight economic times.

- If paying off your mortgage early is the goal, sending one or two extra mortgage payments each year or a little bit more every month to the lender can save you many years of payments and shave off thousands of dollars in interest. *Write a separate check and state on the check and on an accompanying note that this payment is to be applied to the principal balance only.* Verify that the payment was applied to the principal. You could cut your number of payments by about one-third.

- Get out there and buy a property! Even if all you do is break even on the first deal, you will have learned a lot and broken the ice. Getting started is the hardest part.

Know When Real Estate Is Priced Right

How do you know when real estate is priced right? Here are some general rules of thumb.

For single-family homes, pay no more than 100 times the monthly rent that you can comfortably charge. Or, ten times the property's annual net income—rent income less taxes, insurance, utilities and maintenance, including garbage and snow removal, association fees, etc. Do not count mortgage payments.

Single-family homes have value as homes and as shelter, thus, single-family houses tend to cost more than apartments per square foot. And, therefore, single-family houses are a less profitable buy (i.e., they produce less return).

On the flip side, single-family houses are easier to sell, easier to finance, and appreciate faster. When I buy a single-family home, I am looking for a long-term hold (five or more years), or I am buying fixer-uppers at half the repaired appraised value.

For other income-producing property (apartments, offices, and the like), the typical way to figure the property's value is to take the property's net annual income and multiply it by ten. (Do not forget to deduct a five percent management fee for yourself as an expense item). If the property is very nice, very well maintained, in a very nice area, with a very high occupancy rate, you can pay twelve times the annual net.

These rules of thumb will tell you when you have a likely candidate, a good deal. Using these rule numbers, the professional investor will make an offer conditioned upon a due diligence analysis of the income and expense numbers and a property condition report. The final offer will be for ten times the property's current (verified) net income, less any and all repairs needed (remember: repairs should always be estimated at licensed contractor prices,

Every extra $1 of net income equals $10 in property value

regardless of whether you eventually pay that). If you can get the property for less than that number, you should have an excellent bargain.

After you buy the property, make all the needed repairs, spruce up the overall appearance of the property, and get rid of the problem tenants; this repositions the property for higher rents. Every dollar of increased net income adds ten dollars to the property's overall value.

Options to Buy

Buying real estate by exercising an option

An option gives you the right to buy or sell something of value at a future date. The following story will serve to illustrate the use of an option when purchasing property.

Having sold a property, I was looking around for another property to buy. I found a 10-acre unimproved (vacant, with no buildings) property for sale for $240,000 that came with the right-of-way for a road. I would need to put in the road and a sewer line in order to develop the property. I offered 10 percent down with seller financing for two years at five percent interest, payments to be interest only for the two years. The offer, I indicated, was contingent on my property being sold. The seller accepted but also countered with an option for me to buy it for $228,000 cash.

As it happened, the contract with my buyer fell through, which meant I lacked the downpayment to close the land deal. I still wanted the 10-acre property, so I proposed a one-year option to buy at $240,000 with 10 percent down on a two-year, owner-carried note at five percent interest, and I proposed paying $6800 for this option. The $6800 would be deducted from the sales price, I said, if the option was exercised, and forfeited by me if the option lapsed.

I liked the property because the area was beginning to grow; it had some highway frontage, and the road would provide full access to all 10 of the acres. That meant I could re-plat (subdivide) the property into smaller lots, making it suitable for warehouse use, and lease the highway frontage for car or other outdoor sales. By adding the sewer line, doing the re-plat, improving the ingress, and extending the other utilities, the property's value would increase.

Meanwhile, I would gain by using an option to tie up the property while I raised the downpayment. During the option year, I could firm up my plans for the property. I would also avoid the payments, taxes, and interest I would have had to pay up front had I purchased the property immediately.

The seller stood to gain by accepting the option because he would get a $6800 payment for the option essentially risk-free and would get his full asking price if and when the deal closed a mere year or so later. He had a motivated buyer serious enough to risk the $6800 option payment.

How did I arrive at the $6800 figure? It happens to be equal to the property owner's annual tax bill on the property. The offer I made was sold to the seller by explaining that, when the deal closed in a year, the seller would get more than if he had sold the property outright at the $228,000 cash price he'd suggested—he'd get virtually his original asking price. This was true because $228,000 plus a year's interest, plus the $6800 tax bill would add up to just under $240,000.

CHAPTER SEVEN

GETTING THE MONEY TO INVEST

It takes money to make money.

Too true. Over the centuries, this problem has been the primary reason why more people have not become rich. Today, we are lucky in the developed world, in that money is more readily available than ever before in our history. Opportunities to invest money and put it to work for you are also much more abundant.

It takes money to make money...but it doesn't have to be your money

Let's talk now about how to raise the necessary money to get started. Most of us have access to more money than we realize, but we do not thoughtfully plan the use of our money, or know how the money that passes through our hands is spent. If getting rich is your goal, then learning how to manage your money is critical. You will need a plan that indicates what you want to achieve, when you plan to achieve it, and how you plan to get there. You can make your plan informal or formal, detailed or vague, but it should be in writing. You will need to refer to this plan on a regular basis in order to evaluate how you are doing in relationship to your stated goals. A lot of us balk at it but those who are rich know how empowering this step is.

In order to know how far you have come, you have to identify the point from where you started. That means you need to prepare a personal financial statement showing your current net worth. And you need to prepare a monthly cash flow statement for your household. You must know where your money is going if you plan to save and invest any of it. For a free personal financial statement form, visit www.sba.gov/sites/default/files/tools_sbf_finasst413_0.pdf.

Building an investment nest egg

The first thing I learned when I tried to save in order to invest was that an individual or family is likely going to spend every available penny. Every plan my wife and I made fell apart as the inevitable surprise expense came up. Every time we tried to economize to reduce our spending, we ended up giving up. Here is how we finally did it.

All extra, unexpected money coming into the household went in to a separate investment savings account (tax refunds, birthday money, insurance settlements, bonuses from work, overtime pay, paychecks from extra jobs, garage sale proceeds, etc.) We started this in 1978 and, by 1981, we had $4800 saved. I had a goal of $10,000, so I sold my car for $6000 and bought an old pickup truck for $700. I now had the $10,000 I wanted to start investing in real estate.

Twenty-five years later, we still invest most of the extra money coming into our household. Pocket change and one dollar bills were accumulated in a jar every day for those surprise expenses that ruin a budget and, if none came up, we used it for vacation money. We took some of the money from our first three years of savings to start a fireworks sales business to keep the extra money coming in and we ran the business for the next 14 years. We worked every July 4th holiday, Christmas and New Year's selling fireworks. *If you truly desire to accomplish your plan, you will find a way.*

Your Credit Rating and Cash

Of all your assets, your credit rating is the most valuable. A good credit rating combined with the knowledge of how to use it to make money is all you need to make yourself rich. Everything else you do just makes it easier (or more difficult) to make money. Protect your credit rating because, once it is messed up, you will spend years rebuilding it, and that time and effort would be better spent getting rich.

To get rich you need a plan and a solid credit rating

Knowing how to use your credit availability is simple: *Borrow only when the money will be used to make money.* There are three exceptions to this rule: borrowing for an education and to purchase your home and a car. Any other debt that is not intended for a profit-making venture is a hindrance to getting wealthy.

Borrowing money

Borrowing money to make money can make good sense. Be certain that you have a plan for paying the money back and a backup plan just in case things do not work out as planned. Most of my borrowing is for long-term investments in real estate, or for inventory for resale in one of my businesses.

Borrow only to make money

For personal use, I will borrow if the item being purchased will last longer than the payments. That pretty much cuts the list to cars, education, large appliances, and home improvements. Even if I can pay cash, I might not if the money can make more than the loan will cost.

All lenders will expect you to put up collateral and have equity in your venture before they will consider the loan.

Note: *Deposit all money borrowed for investment in its own separate bank account.* In order to deduct the interest on the borrowed funds, you will need to show the IRS that the money was used for investments and/or business purposes. A separate account makes this clean and easy to track.

Cash flow

Cash flow is more important than cash on hand. If you have a positive monthly cash flow, you have choices available to you. For example, let's say that, at the end of the month, you have $300 left over after paying all your monthly household expenses. Your choices of what to do with this extra money include: pay a bill, save it, spend it, invest it, or use it to make the payments on a loan for investment purposes.

Your plan or goals should include increasing your monthly net income from all sources so that you have money to invest (a positive net cash flow). Besides your paycheck, look for other ways to increase your income. For example, work overtime, hold a garage sale, buy a rental house, or take a part-time job.

You do not have to accumulate a lot of money to start a business or buy a rental property. You can borrow the money and use your extra monthly cash flow to pay back a loan used for the investment. The more you increase your monthly cash flow, the more options will be available to you.

List all your cash-raising possibilities every year

Do not wait until you find an investment to start looking for the money. Find the money and the money sources first, and then be ready when an investment opportunity comes along.

Let's imagine that you found a home for sale for $50,000 that you feel would bring in $70,000 if it were fixed up. You offer to buy the house, proposing that the owner carry the note.

You get the downpayment using a credit card loan check and make both your standard credit card payment and the additional payment from the cash from your current monthly personal income/cash flow. You fix up the house quickly and resell it to pay off the credit card loan and the mortgage.

To do this type of deal, you need to really know the local housing market and have a positive monthly cash flow from which to make the payments, as well as the ability to get the home quickly fixed up for resale.

Once a year, I sit down and make a list of places from which I can raise cash. What I want to know is: what is the total cash available to me, should the need or opportunity arise? My money source list includes: cash on hand, savings, insurance policy loans, IRAs, credit card limits, lines of credit, friends, relatives, my net monthly cash flow from investments, rentals, and a few more sources. With a ready knowledge of what money is available to work with, I know what I can do when the opportunities arise.

Existing assets

When you prepare your financial statement, you may well discover assets that have loan value, such as your home, other real estate, 401(k)s, annuities, life insurance policies, and many more. As long as your monthly cash flow can handle the payments, these can be good sources of investment money.

Partners and Family Members

Take on a business or investment partner only if you have no other choice. Partners are a source of money—and of problems. I use partners

━━━ ∞∞∞ ━━━
Partner only if it's the only way
━━━ ∞∞∞ ━━━

only when the partner is a silent investor or the duties are separated and well defined. If you take on a partner to get their cash or expertise, you choose the only two valid reasons. Any other reason is an excuse for not assuming the responsibility of your actions. Partnership deals should be set up with a signed, detailed partnership agreement. Be sure to get both your partner's and your partner's spouse's signature, if applicable, on the agreement.

I have used partnerships to buy real estate and to start businesses. I have always ended up buying out the partner. When the partner is a relative, it is even more important that the details and duties be spelled out, and that a buy-out plan be laid out. I never accept a partner unless they can afford to lose their money.

This SBA website has some good information on partnerships: http://www.sba.gov/manage/partner.html.

Traditional Loan Sources

Credit cards – easy access

Today, money is readily available via credit cards to anyone with good credit. If you can manage your money so that you stay out of trouble, the use of credit cards can assist your investment activities. Before you use borrowed money for investing, you need to have a plan as to how you will repay the loan and a backup plan in the event things do not go as planned.

SBA lender information

The SBA website has information on SBA loan programs and loan preparation information. Most SBA loans are bank participation loans where, under the guaranty concept, commercial lenders make and administer the loans. The business applies to a lender for their financing, the lender decides whether to make the loan internally, and, if the application has some weaknesses, whether they will require an SBA guaranty on the loan. The SBA guaranty is only available to the lender, assuring them that, in the event the borrower defaults, the government will reimburse the lender for its loss, up to the percentage of SBA's guaranty. Under this program, the borrower remains obligated for the full amount due.

The SBA website goes into detail as to what they look for in a loan. Most of the loans are for owner-occupied real estate and working capital loans. The SBA sets the requirements that the bank must meet before the loan is guaranteed, thus, the banks require collateral and experienced business operators. The SBA is not a good source for startup funding. The SBA does have some specialty loan programs that might fit your business, however, and therefore the website, http://www.sba.gov/financing/index.html, deserves some time and consideration.

Here is a brief outline of some popular programs.

SBA Express loans: Line of credit and term loans; loans for machinery, equipment, furniture, fixtures, inventory, working capital, and business acquisitions.

SBA 7a loans: Working capital up to seven years, equipment up to 10 years, real estate up to 25 years, and business acquisitions.

SBA LowDoc: Loans for working capital, equipment, machinery, furniture, fixtures, inventory, and business acquisitions and real estate; loans up to $150,000 with less paperwork.

SBA 504 loans: For existing companies with net worths of less than $6 million. Other limitations apply, including a special requirement that the company must create one job for every $35,000 borrowed. See SBA website for details.

Bank loans: Bank loans are normally made to businesses with at least a two-year track record. Banks are cash flow (net operating profit)-based lenders, and look for profitability, collateral, and owner experience. Visit bank websites for an idea of the types of loans available, and the requirements you must meet. Wells Fargo and Bank of America are two national companies pushing small business loans.

Peer to peer lenders: Go to Google and do a search for peer to peer lenders to loan to or borrow money from other investors, like yourself.

Untraditional Loan Sources

Loan brokers

Loan brokers work on commission and can sometimes put a deal together when no one else can. Never prepay a loan broker; they should get paid from the loan proceeds. I have never met anyone who prepaid a broker that actually got the loan. Some loan brokers have access to private money sources that you cannot find any other way. Brokers have a better chance of finding you a loan if the loan is real estate-based. You may pay a higher rate of interest for brokered loans. The paperwork the broker will require is similar to a bank loan.

The best and safest way to locate a broker is to ask your banker friend or accountant. Beyond that, look to traditional sources such as trade magazines, the Internet, and the Yellow Pages.

Owner/seller financing

Always ask for owner financing. If you are buying a business, be aware that at least 90 percent of all businesses sold are partly owner-financed. Real estate is often owner-financed, if for no other reason than to spread out the seller's income tax liability. When real estate is owner financed, the seller can borrow money using the note as collateral and make their payments from your payments to them. If you are buying business equipment, ask the seller to arrange the financing.

Rent to own with right to sublet

When an owner wants you to put up more of a downpayment than you have, try a rent-to-own with the right to sublet. Have a part of each payment apply to the principal of a set future purchase price. If you find a house that you can rent for more than your own rental expense, then this will work. I know people who started their whole real estate investment career with this one.

The owner gets the steady income from your leasing the house and you get to build up money that is applied to the downpayment. Just be sure the numbers work before agreeing to any deal, and put everything in writing.

CHAPTER EIGHT

REAL ESTATE FINANCING

O nce you've got your sources identified for your downpayment, it's time to line up the rest of your financing. Knowledge of real estate financing is of prime importance to your success as a real estate investor. I recommend that you read several books on the subject.

It is not unusual to find more than one method used in a single deal. Each state is governed by laws covering deeds of trust and mortgages. You should familiarize yourself with the laws of your state by reading a textbook such as *Modern Real Estate Practices* (published by state). Most college bookstores stock this.

A mortgage loan consists of two parts: the debt (money borrowed) and the security or collateral (typically the property being purchased) for the debt. The note is the promise to repay a debt, along with any interest. The mortgagor (borrower) executes a promissory note in the amount of the debt. The deed of trust is the document that conveys the property (creates the lien) to the mortgagee (lender) as security for the debt. A properly executed mortgage is a negotiable instrument. The payee, or holder, may transfer his or her right to payment to a third party. Because the notes are secured by the property, lenders can control the risk of lending on real estate. This security allows for flexibility in payment plans, length of loan paybacks, interest rates, and other note provisions.

This flexibility allows for creativity when financing your properties.

There are three theories as to who actually holds title to mortgaged property. The "Title" theory says the mortgagee (lender) gets title to the security interest in the land, but most states adhere to the "Lien" theory that says the mortgagor (borrower) keeps title. There is also a "Hybrid" theory that says the "Lien" theory applies, until there is a default.[1] Transferring the mortgage on the property to someone else can be accomplished through assumption, where the new mortgagor takes on ("assumes") the existing mortgage or by refinancing in that person's name.

The information provided here is not definitive; rather, it is a starting point designed to get you thinking. Before using any method or type of financing, you should research it fully to gain a full understanding of the benefits, costs, and any disadvantages of using that method or type of financing.

Contract for deed (CFD)

This is my favorite way to sell. With a contract for deed, the seller finances the buyer's purchase with a contract that spells out the terms of the loan. The CFD contractually obligates the seller to deliver the deed or title free of liens and encumbrances to the buyer after the buyer has met the terms of the contract. Those terms can be anything the two parties agree upon, subject to state law. Individual state laws govern contracts for deed, so check your state's rules before using these contracts.

Let's say you, a seller, is willing to take a low downpayment. Some potential advantages to the seller in using a contract for deed include the ability to:

---

[1] "Mortgage." *Legal Information Institute.* 17 Nov. 2012. Cornell University School of Law. 19 Aug. 2010 <http://www.law.cornell.edu/wex/mortgage>.

- delay closing costs

- sell with no appraisals or inspections, and at any price

- charge a higher than market interest rate on the loan

- foreclose more easily if the buyer fails to pay

- avoid most normal closing costs

- wrap the new loan over an existing loan, thereby avoiding having to pay any balance owed on the property

- sell the property "as is"

- sell to a non-qualifying buyer

- pay income taxes on an installment-sale basis

The seller can do anything the parties involved agree to, as long as the seller does not violate state law, such as usury laws (as to the interest rate), and executes a valid contract. The contract for deed is recorded at the County courthouse, not the deed itself. The title remains in the seller's name.

Mortgages

Financing sources have not changed much over the years. What has changed is ready access to the lenders via the Internet.

Conventional loan
A conventional loan is one where the lender relies on the ability of the borrower to repay the loan and the security offered by the property. Most

lenders will not lend more than 75 to 80 percent of the value of the real estate financed to hedge against market downturns.

FHA loan

The Federal Housing Authority (FHA) insures loans on real estate made by approved lending institutions. Most of the loans fall under section 203(b), which applies to loans on one- to four-family residences. The FHA sets regulations that govern the conditions that the property must meet and the rules the lenders must follow to have the loan insured. The fact that the FHA protects the lender against loss allows for smaller downpayments, thus, more people can afford homes.

As the rules are reissued from time to time, it is advisable to check with a lender for the latest requirements. The FHA also has other programs for multi-tenant buildings, such as apartments for the elderly.

VA (GI) loan

The Veterans Administration guarantees loans for eligible veterans. Approved lenders follow the VA guidelines when making the loans. VA loans cover one- to four-family residences. Non-veterans can assume VA loans, but the veteran remains liable unless the VA approves a release of liability.

PMI (private mortgage insurance)

Private mortgage insurance is available to allow a borrower to obtain a mortgage of up to 95 percent of the appraised value of the property. Lenders of conventional loans often require the buyer to obtain PMI when making smaller than customary downpayments in order to better protect themselves against default.

Purchase money mortgage

A purchase money mortgage is a note and deed of trust, or mortgage, given by the borrower as part of the purchase price of a property. It may be a first or second lien note and, in the event of foreclosure, gives the lien priority over judgments against the borrower and any homestead exemptions.

Open-end mortgage

An open-end mortgage loan allows the borrower to secure future advances of funds against a credit limit set by the lender. Home equity credit lines operate like this.

Package mortgage

A package mortgage covers the real estate plus any fixtures and appliances on the property.

Wraparound mortgage

This type of financing allows a borrower to obtain a new, often larger mortgage on a property with the lender/mortgagee agreeing to pay off the existing (underlying) mortgage(s). Some owner-financed deals are done this way. Due on sale clauses in most mortgages have rendered the availability of these "wrap" mortgages scarce.

Blanket mortgage

A blanket mortgage covers more than one parcel or property. These are used to finance subdivision developments or when the borrower is pledging more than one property to secure a loan.

Balloon mortgage

Balloon mortgages offer lower payments initially, with a catchup or balloon (large, lump sum) payment due at an agreed upon date, either during or at the end of a mortgage term. These are generally to be avoided; if unavoidable, plan for it with care, as you run the risk of losing a property if you lack sufficient money to cover the large one-time payment. A balloon payment typically requires you to pay the balance of the loan after a certain number of discounted payments have been made.

Other types of loans

- Assumptions (taking on, i.e., "assuming," an existing loan on the property being purchased)

- Sale leaseback (the seller leases the property you've purchased, usually for the long term)

- Contract for deed (the seller accepts purchase price to be paid in installments, retaining title until the price is paid in full but allowing the purchaser full use of the property from time of contract)

- SBA (Small Business Administration-generated loans)

- Rent to own (renting a property with the option to purchase at a fixed price by a designated timeframe; ideally, a portion of the rent goes toward the downpayment.)

Property owners (sellers) may now be more inclined to carry the financing on their properties. If a seller is looking at the funds received from the property sale to produce income for them, your mortgage payments could give the seller a better return on their money than they can get anywhere else, in addition to tax savings.

Seller-carried financing allows you the most flexibility. The creativity is a matter of the contract clauses and terms to which you agree. A lot of sellers will let you provide the paperwork, which gives you the most control. Let's review some finance contract clauses for mortgages featuring seller-provided financing to give you some idea of what can be done. As we detail various real estate deals, you will come to better understand how some of these options work.

Payments

Payments vary, subject only to what you agree upon. You could have a loan that pays out the principal and interest over a term of 10, 15, 30, or any number of years. You can do a 20-year amortization with a five-year balloon payment. You can do an interest-only loan, with no payment toward the principal (meaning a very large balloon at the end of the entire principal amount). Or you can structure a small payment in the beginning, increasing at set intervals (which may still create a negative amortization, meaning you haven't made a dent in the principal owed). You can include or exclude taxes and insurance escrow payments. You can set the first payment to start at any point or during the term and on any day of month you prefer.

Prepayment

You want to always insist upon a no-prepayment penalty clause—you want to be able to pay off the mortgage at any point should your situation change, without paying a penalty. I have agreed to prepayment clauses only when I was absolutely convinced that I would hold the property long term.

Interest rate

You can set the interest rate at whatever the other party and you agree to. If rates on bank savings accounts are low, you can suggest the seller carry the note, because they can make more from you than from alternative investments. You, as the borrower, might even get a lower rate than possible on a conventional loan.

Points
There is no value to paying points.

Variable interest rates
Fixed-term loans at a low interest rate are best for you as the buyer. If you firmly believe interest rates will drop, however, a variable rate tied to a national indicator (like the prime rate plus one percent) can work to your advantage.

Late fees
Never agree to late fees, unless you are the seller; then, always insist upon this clause.

Tax and insurance reserves
Most owners will let you, the buyer, pay the taxes and insurance yearly. This lets you avoid tying up your money in an escrow account, interest free, but it does mean you must be fiscally responsible to set aside sufficient funds to cover these expenses.

Wraparound mortgage
This type of loan can be used when there is no "due on sale" clause contained in the underlying mortgage and the seller wishes to control the underlying mortgage. The buyer makes payments to the new lender (or seller, if owner-financed), and the new lender (possibly the seller) makes the payment on the old loan. The total amount of the new wraparound loan includes the existing loan's balance, and the principal above and beyond that is owed to the seller.

EXAMPLE

You have a house for sale with an existing mortgage note at six percent interest, with no "due on sale" clause. You sell the house for more than you owe, with the buyer giving you a wraparound mortgage at eight percent interest, this time with a "due on sale" clause. You collect on the new loan and keep making your existing payments instead of paying it off. Some of the benefits to you of using a wrap mortgage in this example are that your buyer is paying you at a higher interest rate, allowing you to make money on the interest rate spread; you can report your taxes on the sale's profits to the IRS using the installment sale method; and your buyer cannot resell without paying you off (the due on sale clause) so that you can then pay off your underlying loan.

This works well when the buyer wants to make a low downpayment and cannot qualify for a regular mortgage. For the buyer, it can solve a finance problem. For the seller, this type of loan can create extra profits because of the interest rate spread.

If you buy a property with a wraparound mortgage, have your attorney check the contract first. You will want a clause that allows you to make the payments directly to the existing loan holder if the seller fails to keep the payments up to date to avoid risking default.

Assumable mortgage

If you find a house with an existing mortgage at a low interest rate that is assumable, you should take over that note and get a new loan for the difference between the existing balance and the purchase price less downpayment. This works best when current interest rates are high and the rate on the underlying mortgage is less than you could ever hope to obtain.

Trade

A like-kind trade delays any income tax due on a sale. Always check with your CPA before doing a trade to protect your tax position. Trades must be handled by a third party. If you do the trade wrong or miss the time constraints, the IRS will want the taxes paid—and you'll have to pay them.

EXAMPLE

Let's say you are in the 20 percent tax bracket. Of every dollar you make on a sale, 20 percent goes to Uncle Sam. You want to sell a property for $100,000 that has an 80 percent building-to-land ratio. You have taken all the depreciation on the building and, if you sell, you will owe taxes on the $80,000 at 20 percent, namely $16,000. That money will no longer be out there making you money. Solution? You trade the property for a higher priced property *to keep all of the money working for you.*

In a two-way trade, you find a property you want and trade with the seller. They take over your property and mortgage, and you take over their property and mortgage, and you give them a note for the difference if the property you're buying is more highly valued. Trades do not have to be between one buyer and one seller. You could do a three-way trade.

Trade for non-real estate items

You can take anything in trade when selling, or give anything in trade when buying. Keep in mind, the IRS will consider the receiver as having gotten "boot," which is defined as cash or cash equivalent or non like-kind property added to a transaction to make an exchange equal, and will consider a trade as a taxable event unless the traded property is 25 percent or less of the total fair value of the exchange.

Creative financing

There are many creative financing scenarios involving real estate deals. The idea is to identify what each party needs and work a deal that gives everyone what they want. When you deal directly with the sellers, you can be creative. When a real estate sales agent is involved, they tend to get in the way, as they will always want to protect their sales commissions.

EXAMPLE

You find a property you want and the seller wants to be cashed out. You have very little money for a downpayment and cannot get the bank to agree to finance you with just a small downpayment. Try to get the seller to remortgage the property without a due on sale clause. The seller then sells the property to you on an owner-carried basis. Your payments to them cover their note payment. You can sell this idea by reminding the sellers that they will postpone part of the taxes they would owe on an outright sale.

EXAMPLE

You find a property where the owner is tired of being a landlord. The purchase requires a new loan to give the seller his equity and pay off the existing mortgage. You propose a lease/purchase with a very small downpayment. You intend to refinance after you build up enough equity to cover the required downpayment. Or, you propose a wraparound mortgage with the seller collecting from you, while they continue to pay the existing mortgage. Alternatively, their bank can arrange to handle the monthly payments and you pay enough to cover the extra bank service fees.

The possibilities are as varied as the properties you have to choose from and the people you will deal with. Each party involved in a deal has wants and needs. Establish what they are and then find a way to give them what they want in a manner that accomplishes your goals. Every problem that comes along is nothing more than an obstacle to be overcome.

Zero down

Zero-down deals can be done. I recommend them only for experienced property investors. After you are confident in your ability to evaluate the investment potential of a property and know with reasonable certainty what you plan to do in order to carry the debt without defaulting, by all means use maximum leverage. I only caution that you not risk the success of your overall plan. If you are not comfortable with a deal, don't do it. I use this question as my acid test:

Will I lose sleep over this deal, or worry if I did the right thing?

My advice about the zero down deal is to think twice before committing.

Ways to do zero-down deals are as varied as the people involved and the circumstances:

- Use a credit card for the downpayment

- Get the seller to carry the full price

- Use equity in another property to get the money for the downpayment

- Get an investor to put up the money

- Look for sellers who want someone to take over the payments of their property

- Look at the foreclosure list at the County courthouse and talk to the lenders about taking over the note before the sheriff takes over the sale

- *Think!* Be creative. A motivated seller and a motivated buyer are all that is needed.

IRAs

You can use individual retirement account savings to finance your real estate investing—consult your CPA on the rules and procedures to avoid IRS penalties and taxes. It can be done using a self-directed IRA.

For more examples of actual, firsthand real estate deals, visit http://www.towardswealth.com/node/79.

CHAPTER NINE

SALES CONTRACT

If you inspect, you will get what you expect.

Contract for sale

Most real estate agents use a standard contract approved by the applicable state. Be sure you read it each time and check for the clauses outlined below.

If the seller's attorney prepares the contract for sale, you should have it reviewed by your attorney. It is advisable to have all contracts reviewed by your attorney prior to signing.

Helpful real estate contract clauses

I have found the following contract clauses can be of help in avoiding problems.

"...or the appraised value, whichever is less."

Add this phrase to the contract sales price area: "Buyer agrees to purchase for [price offered] or the appraised value, whichever is less." This clause has saved me money the few times that a property's value came in below what everyone thought the value should be.

"This contract is subject to approval by..."

Add to every purchase contract: "This contract is subject to approval by [name]." Name a friend or type of firm, such as structural engineer or your contractor. This clause allows you to back out of a bad deal if your named person does not approve the deal.

"This contract is subject to a remodeling or repair estimate from [name], acceptable to buyer."

If you do not feel comfortable with your own repair estimates, then this clause will let you back out of the deal if the cost estimates from licensed contractors get too high.

"This contract is subject to a phase one environmental study unless waived in writing by the buyer."

If there is any question about the presence of lead paint, asbestos, chemicals, or other contaminants, spend the money to have a study done. You do not want to buy someone else's environmental problem. Commercial deals that are financed will require a phase one environmental report.

"This contract is subject to a survey satisfactory to the buyer."

This is money well spent. You do not need to find out later that the fence the prior owners installed is on the neighbor's property, or that the lot is smaller than you bargained for. This can be paid by either party, so try to negotiate who pays, or split it.

Downpayment
Affirmation of what amount the seller demands, even if it is zero down.

Proration of rents and deposits
When buying a rental property, you want a clause covering the proration of rents, security deposits, utility bills, and interest owed on security deposits to ensure you receive income you're due and aren't subject to paying expenses you shouldn't. Check the contract that the real estate agent uses for this clause.

Certificate of occupancy
Verification of the existence of a current certificate of occupancy ensures the building is in compliance with local laws.

Condition of property
This is where you list all inspections you may want, and anything you want the seller to do. Allow yourself sufficient time here until closing to schedule and obtain the necessary inspections. For example, "This contract is subject to a [pest/radon/mold, etc.] inspection and report acceptable to buyer."

Termite inspection
Insect infestations can be expensive to remedy. A termite/pest inspection should be required.

Radon gas and mold inspections
Have clauses added to allow for inspections for both radon gas and mold. For example: "This contract is subject to a [radon/mold] inspection and report acceptable to buyer."

Repairs

Any repairs that are necessary can be deducted from the price for you to address after the closing. (Unless you are buying "as is.") Ensure you obtain estimates from licensed contractors. You are not obligated to use those contractors if you can have the repairs done more cheaply and as competently either yourself or with another firm later on, but you want to be sure you are covered for the entire potential cost.

Inclusions

List on the contract anything that can be removed that you expect to stay. For example: portable storage rooms, ceiling fans, appliances, etc. Request the right to reinspect the property 24 to 48 hours before closing to be sure all contracted property is still intact.

Utilities

Whenever possible, have the utilities transferred to your name a day or two prior to closing. You want to avoid the utilities being cut off and a delay in getting them back on.

Title insurance

The seller should provide you with a title insurance policy. This policy compensates you if the title is later contested. The insurance company will have to defend the title or pay off on the policy amount. This is not required on owner-financed deals, however, I always get title insurance even if I have to pay for it myself. You do not want to find out after the closing that someone else has a claim to ownership.

Risk of loss

Be sure the contract states that the seller is responsible for any losses incurred until after the closing. Have your property insurance take effect the day of closing.

Insurance

Be sure your insurance policy covers the house from the closing date onward and that you have an additional million-dollar liability policy.

Occupied houses or apartments

If you are buying a building with tenants already in it, insert a due diligence clause that allows you to check all leases, rental applications, and tenant background checks prior to closing. Add a clause, too, that calls for the current owner to have any tenants currently in arrears on their rent removed from the building prior to closing. Verify all rental amounts with the tenants and all expenses against the actual bills.

Hazards

Insert a clause demanding that any hazards to health, or that could cause injury, are fully remedied prior to closing, unless you are willing to assume the risk. These would include removal of such things as old cars, repair of unsafe basement doors, etc. Your property inspector should point out these items.

Zoning: flood area

Check or ask the seller to certify that the building is not in a flood zone. (Also, most insurance policies these days do not cover flooding, unless you specifically request it.)

Prepayment penalties

Prepayment penalties greatly reduce your flexibility in selling or trading the property later. Avoid them by ensuring there are none listed in your contract (unless you are the seller and want the interest from a note you are carrying back).

Due on sale clause

This clause is found in most real estate financing documents. You DO NOT want a due on sale clause if you are the buyer. These clauses allow the note holder to require you to pay off the note if you sell the property. Without this clause, you can sell the property with a wraparound mortgage. You can trade the property, with the new buyer assuming the old loan. As a buyer, due on sale clauses give you minimum flexibility and greatly restrict creative financing.

As a seller, however, you DO want the due on sale clause!

Escrow payments

Avoid escrow accounts for taxes and insurance whenever possible. Escrow accounts allow someone else to use your money virtually for free.

Points

Paying points on a mortgage is always negotiable, so ask for fewer points than requested or none at all. When you pay points, you are paying a portion of your interest up front. Each "point" equals one percent of the amount of the loan.

Condominiums and townhomes

Have your attorney check over all the paperwork when buying into a cooperative unit, starting with the offer to purchase. Condos, townhomes, and co-ops all have underlying agreements covering common areas, common walls, garages, gates, use restrictions, and common area expenses. You will find that you are restricted by the rules and covenants of the governing body. Be sure you know what you are agreeing to and what it will cost.

Property appraisals

With owner (seller) financing, property appraisals are not mandatory. I do them anyway, unless I know for certain that the property is undervalued and obviously a good deal. (Other common inspections, such as for termites, are also not required.)

Without a property appraisal, the seller can sell the property for any price agreed to (which can make the more knowledgeable party in a transaction some money).

If you sell a property and the buyer gets a new loan from a mortgagee demanding an appraisal, it caps the price you can get. If you carry the note yourself, on the other hand, you can set the price at anything the buyer is willing to pay. The same is true for terms and interest rates.

Closing costs

Either party can pay the closing costs, or you can negotiate that they be split in any way that suits both parties. With owner financing, there is less paperwork, and the closing costs are lower. The closing is also faster.

CHAPTER TEN

UP TO AND CLOSING THE DEAL

Y ou have decided to buy your first property. Now what?

The following is a description of the generic closing process and what to expect. Each state has slightly different procedures and requirements and it is up to you to familiarize yourself with the particulars of each state in which you are buying. Closings are designed to serve the interests of all the parties equally. A title company or attorney most often handles the real estate closing.

The closing agent, title company, or attorney will follow the laws of the state, the instructions as given in the sales contract, and the instructions given in the loan documents. The goals of the closing agent are to conduct the closing as instructed, to complete the paperwork in a manner that protects the interests of all parties, to handle the disbursement of funds, and to record the documents.

Title to the property and possession always transfers at closing and never before.

I suggest you ask a title company or obtain online blank copies of a standard closing statement and an "Offer to Purchase" contract. Alternatively, you can pick up a copy of *Modern Real Estate Practices* at a college or other bookstore.

Note that you can obtain an estimate of your closing costs from either the title company or closing agent at any time during the process.

Offer to purchase

The offer to purchase is made in writing. It might also be called a "residential earnest money contract," "contract for sale," or something similar. Each real estate sales contract may be different. *Read it!* (See chapter nine regarding recommended clauses to include and avoid.)

The closing agent will follow the contract instructions. The signed contract, along with a check for the earnest money (the amount deposited to confirm a contract), is placed with the title company or closing agent handling the closing. The agent will deposit the money into an escrow account on your behalf.

Real Estate Settlement Procedures Act

The Real Estate Settlement Procedures Act (RESPA) and your state's real estate settlement laws dictate the general procedures and disclosure practices. These laws are designed to protect the buyers *and* sellers, and assure that the settlement costs are disclosed. For more information on RESPA, visit http://portal.hud.gov/hudportal/HUD?src=/program_offices/housing/rmra/res/respa_hm.

The closing agent

The closing agent conducts the proceedings and calculates the settlement and division of charges between the parties as provided for in the sales contract.

Real estate agent

The real estate agent (if there is one) is paid at the closing by the disbursements of funds as agreed to in the contract between the parties. The real estate agent will work with the closing agent and the parties involved to handle any practical matters, such as the results of termite inspections, surveys, needed repairs, etc., to ensure the closing goes smoothly.

Lender

The buyer is responsible to obtain any necessary financing for the purchase. The financing is, or can be, handled by the seller, a lending institution, and/or the real estate agent, if they are assisting in the loan procurement, or if the buyer secures the loan independently. The lender works with the closing agent to ensure proper documentation of the disbursement of funds and the recording of loan documents and property liens.

Title

The sales contract usually requires that a title search and removal of any objections ("clouds") to the title be completed by a certain time. The seller is required to show that he or she owns the property by securing a title commitment or abstract of title from the title company. You should always request title insurance to protect yourself from unidentified liens and other claims when buying a property.

Survey

A survey of the property will provide assurances of the legal description, location, and size of the property, as well as any easements or right of ways that have been granted. I always get a survey (although not always before closing). If the deal is a really good one and if I do not need to be concerned as to exactly where the property lines are, I might decide to wait rather than delay the closing. As a general rule, it is best to survey the property, even if the seller will not pay for it. It is cheap insurance.

Inspection

In the time between contract and closing, you will have inspected the property and determined what, if any, repairs need to be done. Further, you will have negotiated with the seller regarding who is responsible to effect the repairs. I prefer to get more money from the seller at closing to cover the repairs that have been quoted by registered contractors and take responsibility for doing them myself for two reasons: I can get the best value for my money by shopping bids or doing the work myself, and I care more about the quality of the repairs than the seller likely does.[1]

It is important to have the property inspected again just before the closing to ensure there have been no adverse changes to the premises or contents that are part of the sale have been removed.

---

[1] Martinez, Matthew A. *2 Years To a Million in Real Estate.* New York: McGraw-Hill, 2006.

Escrow

Escrow is a method of closing a real estate transaction where the documents, real estate, money, and securities deposited are handled by a disinterested third party (escrow agent). This is often the title company, which is authorized to coordinate the closing activities. In most states, the escrow agent is licensed and bonded. The contract and earnest money should be handed over to the escrow agent upon execution of the sales contract to deposit into an escrow account until the closing date.

Proration

Proration is the dividing up (balancing) of the financial responsibilities related to the property between the buyer and seller. Proration may include taxes, interest on assumed loans, rents, deposits, utilities, insurance, and items particular to the property being purchased.

EXAMPLE

If you buy a rental house with a tenant living in it, the advance month's rent paid by the tenant to the seller would be partially or wholly credited to the buyer's account for the remainder of the month from the closing date to the renter's next due date. This is why I like to schedule closings just a few days after rents are due. If rents are paid on the first of the month and I close on the third or fourth day of the month, I am entitled to virtually all of that month's rent, even though it was paid to the seller prior to closing date (which provides me with income to offset my first mortgage payment).

Closing statement

The closing statement is the document that spells out the charges and disbursements as they are actually made. The closing statement shows a summary of both the buyer's and seller's transactions. It also shows the cash exchanged between the parties. All settlement charges will be listed. You will use the settlement statement in preparing your income tax returns. The settlement statements and all closing documents should be saved for at least five years after disposal of a property.

The Seller will provide to the escrow agent the deed, title evidence (title policy), any letter showing mortgage payoffs, plus anything else required by the real estate sales contract.

The Buyer will provide to the escrow agent the balance of the cash downpayment, mortgage papers (unless it is a cash deal), an insurance policy on the property, plus anything else required by the real estate sales contract or the lender.

Expenses

In addition to the payment of the purchase price and proration of taxes and interest, other charges are involved. These may include:

- Broker's sales commission – seller's expense

- Attorney's fees – either party's expense

- Appraisal fees – either party can pay for a property appraisal

- Survey fees – traditionally a buyer's expense if a new mortgage is being issued.

- Recording (filing) fees – usually a seller's expense.

- Transfer tax – usually a seller's expense, but can be split

- Title expense – usually a seller's expense

- Loan fees (points) – usually a buyer's expense; sellers may also bear points and/or prepayment fees.

- Tax and insurance reserves (escrow) – a mortgage company may require escrowing for future taxes and insurance costs to ensure the bills are paid to avoid potential liens.

Who pays for what expenses will be outlined by the agreement made between the parties in the real estate sales contract prior to closing.

CHAPTER ELEVEN

AFTER THE CLOSING

Now that you own it...

Once you take title to the property, you need to get it ready to lease or sell as quickly as possible.

Home Improvements that Pay

When I first started buying rental houses, my wife and I did all the repairs and painting. We now hire a person to do the labor, and we provide the materials, which is much faster than getting bids and waiting for subcontractors to finish up other jobs ahead of ours. Having control over the labor gets the job done faster. Time is money in the rental business.

One of the most common mistakes that beginners make is to over-improve a property.

- You only want to do the repairs and improvements that will get the place ready to rent or that will help sell the house.

- Do only the work that will get you more at resale than you paid to have the work done, or those repairs that you must do to protect the asset.

EXAMPLE

If the roof leaks, you must at least patch it or replace the minimum amount required to repair the leak, but electing to install designer shingles will not return the premium paid over the cost of basic shingles.

When an appraiser values a home, they start by researching "comps," the selling prices for comparable properties in that neighborhood in order to establish a current market value. They then deduct the cost of those repair and replacement items the home needs, like a new roof, and add anything the home has that increases value, like quality landscaping. They continue this process until they reach their best estimate of the home's market value.

Keep good records of all amounts spent on replacement and repair, as these are tax deductible and/or will reduce your cost basis when you resell.

Protect the asset

When you made your offer to buy the house, you ideally allowed for all the repairs the home needed at contractor rates. You then do the work yourself or subcontract out the work for less, thus gaining the "sweat equity." Start by doing those repairs that *must* be done: foundations, roofs, leaks, mechanical repairs, etc. These are the repairs that are imperative to protect the home and make it usable. *They do not increase the home's value.*

Three areas that will help you rent or sell a house and therefore warrant your investment are curb appeal, bathrooms, and kitchens.

Exterior

Clean the gutters; paint the exterior if necessary; consider a new color scheme if it would greatly enhance the curb appeal. Replace torn screens or anything that appears shabby.

Landscaping

A quick way to turn a few hundred dollars of expense into a few thousand dollars of equity, trim the bushes and trees, replace dead or diseased plants, and clean up the flowerbeds. Color helps. Simple landscaping goes a long way toward increasing property value.

Fences and driveways

Although they do not add value necessarily, they can diminish value and curb appeal. Make repairs when possible, rather than replacing, which can be expensive. If they are in poor condition, be sure to obtain estimates and negotiate a lower price when you buy the property so that you can afford to improve them.

Kitchens and baths

They should be in good repair and very clean. If the bathrooms and kitchens are shabby and/or dated, you will have obtained estimates and negotiated deducting them from your purchase price. If you decide to make improvements while repairing, be modest in the amount you spend.

EXAMPLE

One of the houses I purchased needed a new vanity mirror. The existing mirror was an old, recessed, metal medicine cabinet. I had the option to replace it for $19, buy a triple mirror model for $69, or buy a lighted model for $179. I chose the $69 option as it improved the look of the bathroom at a reasonable cost. I did not do any more than that because fancier mirrors don't add appraisal value.

Interior paint

When painting, stick to neutral colors: beige, tan, cream, and off-white. Lighter colors make the rooms feel larger and will complement most furniture. A fresh coat of paint goes a long way toward giving the house a clean look and feel. Painting one wall a complementary color is an inexpensive way of adding style to a room. Visit model homes for ideas on accent walls and colors.

Appliances

People expect modern appliances that work, with all knobs and handles intact. I buy used appliances when replacing, as the added cost of new appliances will not increase the rental income. When reselling, I deliberately omit the refrigerator and then throw it in as a deal clincher. Stainless steel appliances are expected in houses over $100,000.

Closets

If you are painting the room, paint the closet interiors a lighter shade as it makes them look larger. Add a new 100-watt light bulb to walk-ins. If you are going to sell the home, a mirror on the closet door never fails to please.

Check everything else

Look the home over for anything needing repair and anything that might be a hazard before leasing or reselling.

As a landlord, you are responsible for the houses you rent being safe. When contemplating a repair or improvement, always ask yourself:

1. Is this repair necessary to protect my investment or reduce a hazard?

2. What is the most economical way to make the repair or improvement?

3. Will this increase the rental and/or resale value?

4. Will this improve the property's appeal to buyers and/or renters?

5. Is this work cost-effective?

6. Do the smoke detectors work? (Install new batteries if the detectors are not hard-wired.)

CHAPTER TWELVE

TROUBLESHOOTING

I think we can all agree that most problems are avoidable. In every business transaction, you make a commitment to do certain things, and the other party makes a similar commitment. If you wish to avoid problems, be certain that you understand what you are committing yourself to before you sign on the dotted line. I suggest you read books on real estate financing, modern real estate practices for your state, and a book on real estate taxes to familiarize yourself with regulations and obligations before negotiating a purchase.

A real estate sales contract is a bilateral contract where each party promises to do something. One promise is exchanged for another promise. The seller promises to sell and convey a property to the buyer and the buyer promises to pay for the property. You avoid problems by understanding what you are agreeing to, and living up to your commitment honorably.

Keep in mind that everything in a real estate deal is negotiable and that any contract clause can be changed or modified prior to execution. You cannot get it if you do not ask.

Avoiding Tenant Problems

The fear of tenant problems is the main reason people avoid investing in rental houses. Most tenant problems are avoidable if you only rent to good tenants. Get a copy of the tenant and landlord rights laws or regulations for your state. Check with any large city's apartment owner's association for any help they can provide.

Every time I have had a bad tenant, it was my fault for having taken shortcuts during the tenant selection process.

In advance of occupancy:

Application
Require that every potential tenant fully complete an application form and verify all the information they provide before you agree to accept them. If the person lies on the application, do not rent to them. Check all of their references, especially their most recent landlord. If they have no rental history, insist upon a cosigner on the lease.

Look online for a company to run background and credit checks for you. Charge an application fee to cover the cost.

Run a credit check
If they have a history of late payments, you will be paid late too, if at all.

Run a police report
Check for criminal history.

Obtain a security deposit

Security deposits are imperative and nonnegotiable. If they cannot afford the rent and deposit up front, how will they afford it later?

Require a written, fully executed (signed) lease

The terms could be six months or a year or more. Explain everything to the tenants, and get all persons over 17 years old who will reside on the premises to sign. Review every clause in the lease with them, and have each page initialed.

Include in the lease:

Late fees

Be strict about receiving payments on or before due dates and include a clause listing a late fee to be charged if rent is not paid on time.

Pet clauses and deposits

Require an additional deposit from tenants with pets, a *very high* pet deposit. $500 per pet is potentially too low.

Parking

Cover parking in the lease to avoid misunderstanding later. If you do not, you may find your lawn has become a parking lot.

Rental fact sheet

Here is an example of the kind of information you want to post at your property for prospective tenants, as well as include in any lease agreement. Providing this onsite reduces demands on your time for information.

Two-bedroom apartment at

[No., Street]

[City, State, Zip]

- Rent $550, based on two (2) adults and two (2) children. Additional $50 per additional person.

- Nonrefundable application fee: $35.

- Security deposit of $300 required.

- Rent is due the first day of each month.

- Minimum late fee of $35, plus five additional dollars per day for delinquencies beyond the 7th of the month.

- No pets, unless approved by landlord, in writing. Pet security deposit of $[amount] required.

- No assigned parking.

- Unit is equipped with [one] air conditioning unit, [one] stove, [one] refrigerator... [List all major appliances and portable features]

- Tenant is responsible for utilities [electricity, gas, heat, hot water, telephone, etc., as applicable].

In addition to the above rental fact sheet items, the standard tenant lease should include some form of the following clauses:

- One [air conditioning/stove/refrigerator, etc.] unit is provided as a loaner to the tenant to be returned to the landlord in good working order at lease end. Serial #: _____ [Individual clauses should be provided for each item.]

- Cable or satellite TV service must be installed by a professional and installation approved by the landlord in advance.

- Trash removal: (e.g., "The city provides one trash can per tenant and the tenant must take it to the pickup point before [time, day].")

- No outdoor storage is permitted.

- Any person staying more than three days is considered to be a tenant and must be named on the lease, have completed an application form accompanied by the standard application fee and appropriate fees paid, subject to background check and approval by landlord. Exceptions must be approved in advance, in writing, by the landlord.

CHAPTER THIRTEEN

RECORD KEEPING

Real estate investing requires that you keep records for long periods of time. You need records to prepare your taxes, determine your profits, and decide what to do with your properties. Plan on keeping records on each property until at least five years after you have disposed of the property. A lot of paperwork is generated during a real estate transaction. Save everything. It will save you time, money, and aggravation over the years you own a property.

Papers and records vary, so, instead of trying to anticipate every item that might cross your desk, I will share how I do my own recordkeeping, and why I do it the way I do. I believe in doing the least amount of paperwork possible to maintain comprehensive records, and in keeping my paperwork filing system simple. I recommend you read the textbook called *Modern Real Estate Practices* (for your state) for some excellent recordkeeping advice, which, as I have mentioned previously, should be obtainable in most college bookstores.

Files

I set up a separate file for each property. This file contains a copy of everything involved in the purchase of that property, i.e., the sales

171

contract, a photocopy of the recorded deed (the original should be kept in a safe place), closing statement, any loan or other application papers, inspections, surveys, etc. When the file is complete, I put it all in a large envelope and store it in a fireproof file cabinet. (I keep this information forever.)

Each year, I create another file folder for each property and record on the outside of the folder all rents received on that property. On the inside of the file, throughout that calendar year, I put all that year's corresponding receipts for expenses or repairs that pertain to that property. On the inside cover of the file folder, I keep a list of these, noting the date of the receipt, who was paid, why, and how much, just in case a receipt gets lost. At tax time, it is a simple matter to add up the rent receipts and the payouts. (See the section on IRS Schedule E below).

Additional copies of my income tax returns are filed here by the year, as are financial statements.

Checkbook

I have a bank account set up in my name with "rental account" added after my name. I use this account exclusively for rental property transactions. I pay everything possible by check. At the end of the year, I can easily identify where the money went, why, and how much.

Fireproof Safe

I own a safe to keep all deeds, recorded paperwork, and the rental account checkbook. A safety deposit box at a bank would work equally well to store originals of property deeds.

IRS Schedule E

Each year, an IRS Schedule E must be filed, reporting rental income and any losses to the IRS. I find it helps to set up my property records with the same information found on the Schedule E. (Tax software, such as TurboTax, does a fine job of this.)

Remember: Always consult your tax professional when preparing tax documents.

Depreciation

Depreciation is taken on IRS form 4562. Standard depreciation of residential property is 27.5 years, and non-residential real property is 39 years. You can depreciate the buildings, but not the land. Check with your CPA, as parts of the building may be able to be depreciated faster. Similar to component depreciation, cost segregation may permit depreciation on exterior items such as sidewalks, paving, signs, and landscaping, and interior items, such as floor coverings, interior signage, wall coverings, and some electrical and plumbing equipment. The IRS lost a tax case concerning this. You can use this faster method if you keep the proper records. More information on this can be found at www.irs.gov/Businesses/ Small-Businesses-&-Self-Employed/Audit-Techniques-Guides-(ATGs).

If you have a property appraisal, the land's value versus the improvement value is most likely listed in the appraisal report. If you did not get a copy of the report and purchased the property with conventional financing, request it from the lender. (You paid for it). If you do not find a breakdown for the land's value, ask your accountant for the most common percentage used to calculate land value.

Depreciation offsets (lowers) the amount of rent received that constitutes taxable income. When added to the property's expenses, you might have a taxable loss to reduce any earned income.

When you sell a property, you will need to know your cost basis to determine what your taxable profits are. (Always do a tax free trade if you can to postpone the taxes, maybe forever)

Cost Basis = purchase price plus improvements less depreciation and expenses necessary to get the property ready to sell.

cost basis – net sales price = **taxable profit**

For this reason, you need to keep all property records for at least five years after the property is sold. If the property was part of a like-kind exchange (trade), be sure to keep the records for five years after the property you received in the trade is sold.

IRS Schedule C

Schedule C is the IRS form used for reporting profits or losses from a business. This is the form you use to report business use of your home office. When setting up your income and expense record books, if you follow the schedule C format and categories, it makes it easier to fill out the end-of-year tax returns.

CHAPTER FOURTEEN

REAL ESTATE LIMITED PARTNERSHIPS

A limited partnership is a method of raising money that can be used by any type of business. State statutes regulate partnerships, and the sale of limited partnership investments is considered the sale of securities, which is governed by state and federal regulations. Because of this, I recommend you read a good book on the subject and that you do your homework. I would recommend a Nolo Press book, *The Partnership Book*, as a place to start, which can be purchased at www. nolo.com.

Each project is unique and you must develop your own terms and conditions to fit your state's statutes, and the specific needs and requirements of your project. Competent legal counsel is recommended.

As a sample, in Appendix A through D, beginning on page 239, I provide information on all of the paperwork used to structure a limited partnership formed to fund the construction of a self-storage facility, to give you a general idea of how a deal is put together. Each limited partner bought one or more shares, referred to as investment units.

I sold these particular investment units by telling everyone I knew that I was doing a development project using a partnership of investors to fund the project. If a person showed interest, I tried to sell them an investment unit. Each investment packet, including letters and prospectus, was prepared on quality paper and sent out to a potential investor in an attractive presentation folder. The more professional the appearance, the more professional your appearance.

Investment packet documents

Documents include the limited partnership contract, project feasibility study, copies of the property escrow agreement, copies of the investment escrow agreement, state partnership filings, and any other documents specific to the deal.

Followup sales letters

Followup sales letters were sent out every two weeks with the copy reflecting a greater sense of urgency as the offering closing date neared. Followup calls were made to investors as necessary. Raising money is a sales job requiring action on your part to overcome the fears and concerns of your potential investors. Stay vigilant and always follow up!

Avoiding securities laws requirements

You want your limited partnership offering to be considered a Private Placement, to avoid security filing requirements. The easiest way to do this is to limit the number of investors to 10 or fewer if they reside in different states, and 35 or fewer if all investors reside in the same state. You need to file a partnership filing notice in every state where investors reside.

Note: The partnership used in the sample documents that appear in the Appendix is closed, thereby, no solicitation is being made. This information is presented here for educational purposes only. This is not a solicitation for the sale of securities.

CHAPTER FIFTEEN

RETIREMENT INCOME IDEAS

After you make it, it's what you keep that counts.

Here's a different way of looking at your retirement nest egg! Earn 10–20 percent on your money and retire earlier.

Anumber of retired people have found themselves with reduced income from their well-planned retirement investments. With interest on CD investment in the 0.1–2.0 percent range, their money does not provide the extra income they had counted on for their retirement needs.

Most people would prefer to retire in their forties and fifties rather than in their sixties or seventies, and everyone wants to have more money to spend in retirement. It is possible. Here are some lesser known, real estate-based methods of investing your retirement nest egg to produce a better monthly return.

The examples given here are from real-life situations. They are presented to get you thinking about untraditional methods of handling retirement accounts. They should be considered as part of the mix when planning your retirement income. While the suggestions here are conservative, they are not for everyone.

These ideas presume that you are of retirement age, that you want to conserve capital, that you are very conservative, that you are interested in spending very little time in handling your investments, that you want to keep taxes low, and that you want to leave something for your descendents.

The website www.tdameritrade.com/wealthruler has a wealth calculator that will allow you to begin structuring a traditional retirement action plan.

A Rental House Solution

Jerry and Beth's retirement income consisted of Jerry's teacher's pension, Social Security, and $240,000 saved in a taxable annuity. The interest income on their savings had fallen to 3.5 percent, or $8,400 per year. This interest rate of 3.5 percent was considerably less than the average eight percent interest rate they had anticipated. Their home was mortgage-free and they were doing just fine on the income they had.

Any extra income (if they could make more income from their investments), would allow them to travel more and enjoy a few extra luxuries. They were both in their late sixties and would likely need a good income for many more years.

I suggested they consider buying three $60,000 rental homes in a good working-class neighborhood and rent them at $650–750 each per month. That would net them about $550 per house, per month, after taxes and maintenance costs, a total of $19,800 per year in additional income. After buying the homes, they would still have about $60,000 cash on hand as a safety cushion. That would give them a return of about 11 percent on their cash investment.

I explained to them that homes in this price range were readily available in their town and that finding renters in that price range was easy as my proposed rental rate was very competitive. If they did not wish to deal with the tenants, I suggested they hire a real estate agent who specializes in handling rentals on a percentage basis.

The advantages to this proposal included:

- increased monthly income

- tax savings from depreciation

- income inflation protection through increasing rents

- inflation protection of the original investment due to increasing home resale values

- Lowering the risk of long-term vacancy by buying moderately priced homes with affordable rental rates in good neighborhoods

- reducing the risk of a negative cash flow during vacancy by buying the home on a cash basis

If Jerry and Beth did not want to be landlords, they could still use real estate to gain the same increased monthly cash flow without the rental worries. Read on!

Buy Mortgages – Be a Lender

How do you get a 10–20 percent return on your cash?

Where do rich people put a chunk of their money?

Where do insurance companies put a portion of the premium dollars they collect?

The answer is in mortgages purchased on the secondary market. If you have a lot of cash to invest and seek high returns, you can do the same thing these major investors do.

There is a very large market dealing in first and second mortgage notes.

The advantage to this type of investment is that the rate of return is rather high with minimal risk. The disadvantage is that your money is tied up long term and the payments to you include principal as well as interest, requiring you to reinvest the principal part of the payments.

There are brokers who can find mortgages for you to purchase, and some even manage the whole process. You can find your notes to purchase by searching the county records for first mortgage lien fillings, and offer to buy the notes directly from the holders. You could try advertising in the classifieds. You will find mortgage brokers listed in the phone book, and there are always the owners of those signs, "We buy houses." Someone has to finance those deals. Call them; they will love you.

It is possible to get better than a 20 percent return by buying notes at a discount.

EXAMPLE

You find a note where the seller carried a note for $40,000 at 8 percent interest for 20 years. You offer the note holder cash for 90 percent of the balance owed. The note holder gets $36,000 now and you get the payments with interest on the full $40,000, greatly increasing your return on the $36,000 you actually paid out. That would give you an annual return of over 14 percent on your $36,000.

Providing Mortgages Can Make You 10 Percent or More

Proposal: You buy a home for cash at 10 percent below the market price and then resell it (acting as your own real estate agent), and carry the note for the new buyers.

Action Plan: You let everyone know you are looking for a home to buy for cash. Call all the real estate agents in the area where you want to buy and let everyone you meet know you are a buyer. Look for a good, clean, well-maintained house in a working class neighborhood. When you find a prospective property, offer 10 percent under market or less than the appraised value. (See "Real estate purchase contract clauses" below.) The idea is to buy a house at either 10 percent or at least $10,000 less than the current appraised value. After you buy the house, put up a sign "For Sale by Owner, Owner Financing." You resell the home for the full appraisal value and carry the note for the buyer at 8 to 14 percent interest with the enticement of only a five percent downpayment required.

Will people sell for 10 percent below market? Yes! That is because cash buyers are hard to come by. There will always be someone who needs to sell now and will do so at the discounted price. It can take awhile to find the right deal. Be patient and keep looking.

Let's look at what you accomplish with this method. You have an 8 to 10 percent return on **the safest loan you can make**: a real estate-secured first mortgage. You have more than five percent of your cash back. You saved the resale sales commission. You collect 8 to 10 percent interest on the full selling price, not just on the cash you have invested.

EXAMPLE

You buy a home worth $100,000 for $90,000 cash. You sell the home for $100,000, asking for five percent down. You carry the 20-year note on $95,000, payable at $917 per month, principal and interest. (When I carry a real estate note, I collect monthly escrow for the next year's taxes and insurance, as the buyers may not have the discipline to save the money themselves and you don't want to jeopardize your ownership.) Because you only have $85,000 loaned out after the downpayment is accounted for, you get an equivalent rate of return of 11.7 percent annualized. That is many more times the going CD savings rate.

Will people buy at 10 to 14 percent interest? Yes, absolutely! Because of the low downpayment, low closing costs, and easy qualifying, they certainly will.

What if I need money in the future? You can always borrow against the real estate note(s) you hold. Plus, you will be accumulating the payments you are receiving each month. You can always sell the notes on the secondary market.

Real estate purchase contract clauses: I use these two clauses on purchase contracts when I buy property to give me the option of backing out of the deal if a price or property condition problem arises.

1. "This purchase is subject to an inspection by [your home inspector's name here] that is satisfactory to the buyer." This gives you a legitimate way to back out of the deal if the home inspector advises you of any serious problems.

2. "The purchase price will be $[xxx] or 10 percent less than the appraised value, whichever is less." This assures that you are getting a deal on the price. Cash buyers should insist on a deal with this level of incentive. If your real estate agent tells you that this cannot be done, get a new agent.

Paperwork for your buyers: Any good attorney can draw up a mortgage note for you for a few hundred dollars. Spending the money on the lawyer will give you peace of mind, knowing the paperwork was done correctly.

The title company or your attorney will record the liens.

Important finance clause: Add a clause to the note that states that, if the buyer pays off the note during the first five years, they will have to pay you a five percent prepayment penalty. You do not want the property paid off, as the reason you carried the note was to get the steady income.

What if the buyers don't pay? If your buyer does not pay, you foreclose on the loan and resell the home. You will get another downpayment and start the process again. I have only had to foreclose one time and I made money on the deal. Have your attorney do the paperwork and document the condition of the home as well as the cost of getting the home ready to resell.

So, You Want to Retire Early?

To retire early enough to enjoy it, borrow yourself into an early retirement.

When you deposit money into a retirement fund (such as 401(k)s, annuities, IRAs, etc.), the institution holding the money invests that money in income-producing investments. A large portion of that money goes into income-producing real estate investments. The more conservative the retirement fund managers are, the more they will invest in real estate or bonds instead of stocks.

Income-producing real estate is one of the safest investments you can make. Because this type of investment is so safe, banks are willing to lend 70 to 80 percent of the appraised value of the property. Because you can raise rents, you are protected against increasing expenses and inflation. Because of these facts, you can borrow yourself into an early retirement income.

This example assumes you have sufficient money for a downpayment. Let's suppose you go to your bank and tell them you have found a 16-unit apartment building that generates a monthly rental income of $7200 that you want to buy for $640,000.

The banker would tell you that the property would have to appraise for that amount, and you will need 30 percent, or $192,000, as a downpayment. If you can get a 25 percent down loan, you will only need $160,000. There are loan brokers that can get you in for as little as 15 to 20 percent down.

The first thing for you to do is to find out how much cash you can raise by cashing in all of your IRAs, annuities, stocks, life insurance policies, etc. Quadruple the amount of cash you can raise and that figure will tell you how expensive a rental property you can afford.

Start reading books on real estate investing and learning how to evaluate a deal. Keep in mind that there are plenty of professionals who can help you. Once you know how much you can borrow, and how much cash you can raise, start looking for a property that is underpriced because of its cosmetic condition and because the rents are not up at market rates. There are plenty of properties out there that need sprucing up that have rents that have not been increased to market rates.

Do not rely only on real estate agents. Advertise that you are looking. For example, run a classified ad that says "Wanted: 12- to 16-unit apartment building. Fax details to..."

Using our example above, a building that costs $640,000 and has a 30-year mortgage at seven percent interest would require payments of $3000 per month. Assuming you did not raise the rents, you would have a gross income, after making your payment, of $4200 a month.

From that gross income you would pay insurance, taxes, and maintenance. The amount left over is your net operating income (NOI). If the expenses added up to $1500 per month, you would have a net income of $2700 per month. This is a 17 percent return on your $192,000 downpayment!

Spruce up the place and raise the rents 20 percent and your gross income goes to $8640 per month. Less payments, taxes, and maintenance of $4500, and your return goes up to $4140 per month, a 26 percent annual return on your downpayment, cash on cash!

Every time you make an improvement or raise the rents, your property's value increases. Every time you make a payment, your net worth increases by the amount of the principal you paid down.

If you wanted to put cash in the bank at five percent interest and receive the same monthly income of $4140, you would need to make a cash deposit of $828,000.

Think out of the box and you can get very rich.

Here is a federal information center; it is a terrifically informative site about money, saving and investing, retirement, wills, credit and much more: http://www.pueblo.gsa.gov.

For another retirement income option, see the section on Mobile Homes in chapter six.

The Man Who Did Not Sell His Property!

The Tax Man Cometh

Fred has been a general contractor for 40 years. During that time, he purchased a 1.5-acre piece of land and a 6000-square-foot metal building with office space that he used for his business. At age 72, Fred was ready to retire. I met Fred at an auction where he was selling off his accumulated construction equipment and business assets.

I asked if his property, located on a fenced corner lot in an industrial area about 95 percent occupied and with buildings in good condition, was for sale. He asked what I thought the place was worth. I estimated about $360,000. He asked what I wanted it for and I told him I would build another 4000-square-foot steel building with minimum office space and rent out both buildings for the income. He turned me down. Let's look at why.

If Fred sold the property for $360,000, less the selling costs and income tax of $116,000, he would have $244,000 left to invest. At a return of five percent, he would earn $12,200 annually. However, if Fred leased the building for $3000 per month, he would bring in $36,000 per year and still have all of his $360,000 working for him. (I suspected he could get $4000 per month.) As Fred had already depreciated the building to zero, he could not depreciate it again. If Fred built another building to lease out, he would be able to depreciate the new improvements to shelter some of the rental income.

A year or so later, I ran into Fred at a restaurant. He had built the other building and commented that he should have retired earlier and gone into the rental business. He could not thank me enough for the idea.

Too Much House, Too Little Income

Reverse mortgages

Marybeth, age 82, and her husband raised their kids in a fine neighborhood with low crime and easy access to the city's amenities. But, with her husband gone, plus less income from her stock investments due to a long bear market and Social Security reduced to one check per month, her income was not covering all her monthly expenses. Her investment portfolio was shrinking because she was being forced to spend part of the principal each month.

Her home was mortgage-free and worth about $300,000. She was considering selling it and renting a condo, but could not find one that suited her lifestyle and she did not really want to move. I suggested she look into a reverse mortgage at least to cover the monthly cash shortage and the maintenance and other costs of owning her home. A reverse mortgage could provide her a way to stay in her home.

Marybeth and her son investigated reverse mortgages, starting at www. reverse.org, and learned that she could get up to $12,000 per year from her home. The discouraging factor was the high upfront fees.

Marybeth's son decided to be the bank and send his mother $1000 a month with the understanding that he would get his money back, with interest, when the house was sold. She had her attorney do the reverse mortgage paperwork so that there would be no problems when it came time to settle her estate.

She now has her extra income and has stopped the drain on her retirement savings balance. This arrangement will help assure that her savings will not be gone before she is, and she can afford her current active lifestyle while Marybeth's son has a secure first mortgage investment note secured by a home he knows well.

The interest may be tax deductible to Marybeth and taxable to her son, even though it is an accumulation. (Be sure to use an attorney if you decide to do a reverse mortgage, and always check with a tax adviser before entering into any contract.) Visit www.goldengateway.com for a reverse mortgage calculator.

Traditional Retirement Methods

A comment about Roth IRAs

Roth IRAs are the best gift the U.S. government ever gave us citizens. You put **after-tax** money in a Roth IRA investment (Roth IRAs can be invested in a lot of different ways, including real estate). You do not pay tax on the Roth IRA's earnings and you do not pay tax when you withdraw the funds (subject to the Roth IRA rules and restrictions). The money grows without tax liability and is not taxed later. This is a huge advantage. If you do not have a Roth IRA, investigate them. Roth IRAs are a very good deal for everyone with an income under $150,000. For more information, visit www.irs.gov.

The Rule of 72

The rule of 72 is a simple math formula that calculates how many years it takes for money saved at a given interest rate to double.

EXAMPLE

Let's say that you are 30 years old and have $10,000 in a Roth IRA earning 10 percent interest. How much will that $10,000 grow to be worth when you reach age 65?

Take 10 percent and divide it by 72, which gives you 7.2 [years]. Every 7.2 years your money will double if continually invested at 10 percent. Take your retirement age of 65, less your current age of 30, which equals 35 years to retirement. Taking the 35 years you have until retirement and dividing it by 7.2 gives you 4.86 times that your money will double when invested at 10 percent before you reach age 65. Take $10,000 and double it 4.86 times and you get a total of $297,600. That is the magic of Roth IRAs combined with compounded interest. Because Roths are non-taxable, tax liabilities are not considered.

Annuities

Annuities are a common insurance-based retirement investment, and, generally speaking, for anyone who lacks the discipline to save, they are okay. All I have to say about them is there are far better, more profitable ways to invest for retirement.

401(k)s

The next best thing to a Roth IRA is a 401(k). If your employer matches any part of your pre-tax investment, then they are very good indeed. My advice is to maximize your 401(k) investment every year possible. This is a very important asset and you should study the subject. I recently advised my daughter and son-in-law to maximize their 401(k) and reduce their contributions to their Roth IRA to do it. My son-in-law's employer matched 100 percent of his contributions up to three percent of his salary and matched 50 percent of the next two percent. That comes to an 83 percent return the first year on his contributions from the employer's matching alone. Don't ignore this free gift of money.

Employer stock purchase plans

By all means, take advantage of any employer-sponsored plans. I know one employee of Walgreen's drug stores who accumulated a million dollars of stock using the employee stock purchase plan.

Taxes

Before using any of the suggestions provided here, always check with your accountant or other tax professional for tax advice. You want to avoid incurring a tax liability that would reduce your investable cash.

CHAPTER SIXTEEN

GEM REAL ESTATE PROPERTIES, LLC

How I Built a Million-Dollar Real Estate Company

Gem Rental Properties LLC. is my newest company, founded in 2010 for the purpose of investing in rental real estate. The LLC form of doing business is the simplest form of company that allows you to hold properties in other than your own name. You are still liable on the mortgage notes, but transfer of company ownership is easier than if the properties are in the owner's actual name.

The owners of this company are experienced real estate investors, gainfully employed, who do not need to make a living from the LLC company. The goal is to grow a real estate company that will make the owners large sums of money. Anyone wishing to follow along here and do the same is welcome to steal all the ideas they want. Just keep in mind that these are experienced investors, not big risk takers. As experienced investors and businessmen, they are intimately familiar with real estate, accounting, business practices, etc. If you have any concerns as to your experience along the way, consult the necessary professionals.

The following are the general plans and structures under which this company operates.

Gem Rental Properties LLC deals in income-producing real estate, both residential and commercial.

The goal of this company is to earn total returns in excess of 20 percent per year on the invested capital. In addition, we increase equities by improving properties and repositioning them to their highest and best use.

Each property purchase is a Steppingstone to building a real estate investment portfolio worth several million dollars. The first goal is to reach 50 rental units or $1,000,000 in value. That goal will then double to 100 rental units and so on. Each rental unit should produce a minimum of $200 gross positive cash flow per month.

Mortgages on the properties should not exceed 66 percent of the appraised value. This number is lower than the 75 to 80 percent common with rental properties, but it helps assure that the resulting cash flow covers the note payments in the event that high vacancies occur for any extended period. It also reduces the investment risk while allowing for sufficient cash flow for property maintenance.

Properties are chosen after considering the following: purchase price, opportunity for equity improvement, cash flow, risk, cost of rehabilitation or repositioning, availability of financing, and other real estate evaluation factors. We look for properties where we can quickly add to our equity.

Properties are reevaluated after rehabilitation or repositioning for the best use of the property. The considerations include: holding the property for rental income, refinancing to free up equity dollars for another purchase, selling the property, syndicating the property, or trading it.

When we reach 50 rental units, an attendant with handyman skills will be employed to handle the daily operations. At 100 units, an office manager will be employed to handle office operations and rentals.

Once a year, the operation will be evaluated as a whole. Considerations will include whether to continue as before, to consolidate into larger properties where management companies can run things, to sell everything, to hold everything, and other possibilities.

Getting Started

Why am I doing this now? Because I can. And because the bargain real estate deals are out there now. And because, for some time, real estate has been just a so-so investment. And because, when the real estate market is bad, the risk to the investor just coming into the market is actually less, as he is able to buy outright. And because I am a "dirt" man—I have to own it; it's in the genes. And because it is fun. And because it is an opportunity to make more money. *Why?* Because I want to buy even more real estate!

I have years of experience doing real estate deals and I own income-producing real estate. That gives me the confidence and some resources to work with as I start this new real estate investing company.

You have your own resources and contacts to get started with, plus you have this book to teach you everything I know. You also have me telling you what I am doing and how I am doing it to give you the confidence to do something similar.

Money

We started with $12,000 and we are adding more as we go. The amount of money we add each month varies, depending on what we are doing. This method is slower than borrowing money for property repairs, but it reduces risk. As our goal is to refinance our first property as soon as it is rehabilitated in order to free up money to purchase a larger property, we want as much equity in the property as possible. Paying cash as we go adds to that equity.

Raising money is the hardest part of real estate investing. The more you do it, the better you get at it. The more properties and income you acquire, the easier it gets and the more options you have. Raising money will always be difficult, but going through the process sharpens your skills. Learn to think outside the box and consider all sources. For example, some money sources might include: loans, barter, trade, partnering, credit cards, etc.

Innovation

Eventually, after we get to larger properties, we will use less innovation in our property rehabilitation. To start with, we are using barter, partnering, trading, borrowing of equipment, using a credit card for materials, bargain shopping, and calling in favors to get as much done as possible at the least cost. We want to get the rehabilitation done without taking out a second loan.

When you rehabilitate larger properties, you can lose money by trying to be too cheap. You could easily slow down the remodeling and increase the number of vacant units, which would then stop producing income. These alleged savings are then offset by your losses in income. It always comes down to time or money. Saving money takes time. When you get more money and resources to work with, you can speed things up. As a rule, the faster you get the work done, the cheaper it is.

Timing

By my estimates, we have a five-year window to get up to a size that will be self-sustaining. That would be somewhere between one and two million dollars in equities, earning 20 percent per year, and netting at least 15 percent.

There are always bargain-priced properties available, and one need only adjust one's investment strategy to make money. It is not always possible to build equities quickly; to do that requires bargain-priced properties and that takes time and effort. This is just such a time, and I must take advantage of the opportunity now, as I am getting older. These buying opportunities tend to occur about every 10 to 15 years. This is a 5- to 10-year adventure, so it will be my last—and my biggest.

Get started

It's time to get with it. Even if you just do one or two deals, get started. The scary part goes away by the third deal, so get out there and break the ice. Even if you screw things up, the downside risk is only 10 to 15 percent of the purchase price and the upside potential is 20 percent or more.

Good luck

Rich people seem lucky to others, but, in reality, they make their own luck. You cannot get lucky enough to hit a home run unless you first step up to the plate, bat in hand.

Property Worksheet

The property worksheet I use can be found in Appendix E. I fill one of these out on each property to see if the property will fit into our overall plan. I keep one in the file of each property we buy. At the end of the rehabilitation process and after the property has been rented, I redo the worksheet to see if we have hit our goal for the property.

Our First Investment Property – 2010

Five-unit apartment

I made our first investment of the New Year, closing on a five-unit apartment site in late January. There were very good real estate deals available and I expected to do several more deals that year. In order to do so, and as a future business model, I chose to use a real estate LLC.

This property consists of a house and four two-bedroom, one-bath apartments. When fixed up, I originally thought we would have about $105,000 in this project. It turned out to be more along the lines of $130,000. But, I had already decided that **the deal was extra profitable.** Most deals return 15–20 percent a year, in which case, investors would double their money in five years. I estimated the value of this property at about $200,000, which would give us an estimated return with appreciation over five years of 300-plus percent. As it turned out, I was wrong again, happily this time.

We paid $66,000 to purchase the house and four-unit apartment building. The income would be $3000 a month. Our payment, taxes, insurance and utilities came to $1100 a month, giving us a cash flow of $1900 a month. The value of the property after the top-to-bottom remodeling was actually $285,000 instead of just the $200,000 I'd estimated.

This five-unit property was the first project that we undertook in January 2010. The reason we purchased it was to get started—**getting started as soon as possible when you are in the cash flow business is important**. The other reason we purchased this property was because the bank was willing to finance it with only 10 percent down.

We refinanced, taking out $150,000 in cash to buy more properties and to finish the rehabilitation of the four-unit building. The refinance was at eight percent, compounded annually for five years and with no monthly payments, just one balloon payment at note's end. We will have to repay $223,000 in five years, a risky proposition if you're not careful.

We had paid cash thus far to rehabilitate this property. Prior to this infusion of cash from the refinancing, we were paying out of pocket. We were still paying all business expenses out of pocket. We put all incoming cash right back into more projects as this is a five-year plan.

The reason for paying cash for the property improvements was because we wanted the maximum amount of equity available to us when we went to refinance this project. (It's a good example of how it does not take deep pockets to get rich.)

With the equity, we purchased several more properties and a real estate note.

First, we purchased a three-bedroom, one-bath virtually new single-family home with 1056 square feet, no garage, on a 60'x130' lot for $36,000. The home was located in a rural area, on a dirt road south of San Antonio, Texas, and **was a bank-owned repossession (REO)**. We paid 15 percent down, plus closing costs, anticipating spending about $5000 to fix it up. We extended the gravel base driveway, added a chain link fence and a stove and did a few cosmetic touchups. The house was rented to a schoolteacher for $650 a month with a $600 deposit. We had more interest from potential renters on this out of the way house than any other we have ever owned. The key was that it was a new house with three bedrooms for only $650 a month.

After that, we bought **a two-bedroom, one-bath house** that someone had intended to add a room to, but stopped at the shell stage. We wanted to convert this to a four-bedroom, two-bath property that would rent for $900 a month. The cost was $26,000 and we estimated the cost to rehabilitate would be about $20,000.

Following that we purchased a first lien real estate note at a cost of $7500 with a balance owed of $20,000 payable at $350 a month with a balloon note due December 2012.

Then, we purchased a two-bedroom, one-bath house with a one-car garage. We wanted to convert this into a three-bedroom, one-bath property to rent for $750 a month. The cost was $23,000. The cost to rehabilitate would be about $12,000.

Our next purchase was a **three-bedroom, two-bath manufactured (prefabricated) home** of about 1900 square feet on a corner lot. We intend to sell it on an owner-carried note for $92,000 with a $2000–5000 downpayment at 10 or 12 percent interest. The cost was $26,000. The cost to rehabilitate was $33,000.

Assuming we get all of these projects completed, we will have achieved a combined net equity of $385,000.

These properties should produce $6450 a month in income and our net free cash flow should be about $3500 a month. We have spent $48,000 in cash, another $40,000 in trade, and borrowed $249,000.

Our debt-to-equity ratio is 41 percent. Total rehabilitated value of properties and notes equals $605,000. We can borrow another $150,000 and still be at our 66 percent debt-to-equity ratio, enabling us to free up money for more purchases. Three of the six properties are debt-free and can be used to secure new loans. Our return, cash on cash, is 40 percent a year. I am making the assumption that we will complete the projects and get the intended rents. So far, renting has proved easy, and, as I have been doing this a few decades, I am confident of my numbers.

We had hoped to have sixteen front doors at the end of year two of our plan and it looks like we will end up with between ten and twelve. We currently have ten front doors on seven properties (counting the note receivable as one front door). We will need to add twelve or sixteen more front doors next year to stay on track. I place more importance on the free cash flow per front door and the debt-to-equity ratio than I do on just the total number of units rented out.

You make your money when you buy; you gain equity when you rehabilitate; and you need free cash flow in order to grow, as well as to have spendable net income.

The net spendable cash flow is what allows you to keep your loans paid during extended vacancy periods. It allows you to pay for unexpected expenses and generally keeps you out of trouble. When I look at a property to buy, I want to double my money (purchase/downpayment and rehabilitation cost). I want a free cash flow of $200 a month or more, assuming I will borrow up to 66 percent of the improved value at eight percent interest. If a property will produce that, it is considered. So far, we are beating those numbers.

This is a good time to remind you of our five-year project's goals:

- To create $2 million in equity with a net spendable free cash flow of $160,000 a year. (My partner thought it should be $240,000 a year divided by two; I won't argue with that.)

- Each property purchased must produce $200–300 free spendable cash flow a month (per front door).

- The debt-to-equity ratio may not exceed 66 percent.

To give you a more detailed sense of how I break down the numbers to evaluate a property, let's take a closer look at the purchase of that two-bedroom house we bought for $26,000.

If you recall, the cost was $26,000 and we estimated the cost to rehabilitate would be about $20,000. In actuality, the total cost came to $44,000.

Annual Expenses	
Mortgage	3088
Taxes/Insurance	930
Total	4018
Gross Rental Income	7800
Less Expenses	4018
Net Income	3782
Return*	17%

*7800 ÷ 44,000

How do you find great deals? You must look! They are out there, in every price range, and you should always be looking. Talk to realtors; go to investment clubs; pass out cards; talk to everyone; check the real estate websites; drive the side streets; take the back roads home; search online for bank-owned real estate (REOs), etc.

You make your own luck; or, said another way, good luck comes to those who seek it out.

The rich get richer because they work at it.

Purchase: Doublewide Prefabricated Home

Cost: this property was a doublewide manufactured home on a corner lot that we bought from a bank for **$26,000** because the street wasn't so good and the neighbor's place was an eyesore.

Size: the house was about 28'x71' or roughly 1980 square feet. **It had three bedrooms,** two living areas, two-sided fireplace, large kitchen, laundry room, central heating and air conditioning, a large master bath, walk-in closet, and back porch.

Once we repainted it and replaced all of the carpet, this house was impressive. It had a large, open, and very livable floor plan.

Size of yard: the lot was 114 feet along the front, 45 feet at the rear, 103 feet on one side, and 98 feet on the other.

Other information: The property has a septic tank and no garage. The home has sheetrock walls and cathedral ceilings and is approximately ten years old.

Cost of repairs: $33,000. We went over budget by $15,000 on this project because we had to move the house 6.5 feet to solve an encroachment issue ($3200), three trees had to be removed, and we had to replace the AC coil. This was in addition to all of the remodeling and clean up that we had already decided on.

We made the following **additional improvements:** replaced the skirting with new beige prepainted steel skirting, fixed a broken kitchen cabinet door, replaced the base trim at the floor throughout the house, put in new front door weatherstripping, and a handful of little things that one finds as they go through a place.

Outside: We built a privacy fence to define the lot area on the east (back door) side. We put a chain-link fence on the north side. Then we repaired the other fences and built a low 30-foot retaining wall on one side.

We held this house in inventory awaiting rehabilitation because we needed to complete one of our Taft Street houses so that we could refinance it to get the money to do this one.

We will sell this property for $92,000. We will consider financing it for the buyer. It is currently rented at $900 a month.

Should we decide to sell on an owner-carried note, the downpayment would be somewhere between $2,000 and $5,000. The interest rate will depend on the amount paid down (between 10 and 12 percent), and the buyer's credit and job history. Payments will be about $900 a month. Taxes and insurance will add about $100 a month.

Our financing: We will start looking for financing for this house to free up cash for another deal.

Advertising: We ran advertisements on Craigslist to find the tenant and we used on-site signs. Site signs work best on rural properties.

Property Evaluation

Using the property evaluation form found in Appendix E, we calculated the value of this property as follows:

Address:	2281 Contour	Property Type:	Rental Dbl-wide

Purchase price	$25,380
Estimated improvement cost	$33,556
Total estimated investment	$58,936

INCOME	Monthly	Annual
Estimated income	$900	$10,800
Property taxes		$1,158
Insurance		$1,059
5% maintenance allowance		$540
Total operating cost		$1,599
Net operating income		$8,043

Property value

After rehab	$92,000
10% cap rate (net annual income x 10)	$80,043
Property value based on comps	$95,000
Monthly rent x 100	
(Single-family and duplexes only)	$90,000
Amount to refinance (66% of value)	$60,000 at 8% = $471/mo.

Cash Flow

$ Monthly	$ Annually	% Annually*
(all cash deal) $670	$8,043	13%
(financed) $230	$2,760	4% on cost(100% on cash invested if we borrow out all)

*On all cash deal: cash flow ÷ cash invested; with financing, cash flow – mortgage payments ÷ cash invested

Purchase: 340 Taft Street

We purchased this REO property in August of 2011 from a bank for $23,000. It is a two-bedroom, one-bath home, with about 1200 square feet.

We began work on the rehabilitation of the property on November 20, 2011. We originally thought the cost would be around $10,000, but it was more like $12,000. The city made us rebuild the meter loop at a cost of $1400. You can expect more of this requirement as cities upgrade to "smart" meters.

We textured and repainted all of the walls and ceilings. The kitchen cabinets were repainted a cameo white and the countertops were redone in marble green ceramic tile. We removed an extra door that went to a bedroom so that more kitchen cabinets could be added. This also allowed us to add another closet to that bedroom.

The hardwood floors were sanded and resurfaced. The windows were painted and repointed. All of the light fixtures and plumbing fixtures were replaced. Smoke detectors were added. A new hot water heater and a new wall-mounted A/C unit were also added.

Outside, we did repairs to the siding, added a new patio cover, a new garage door, and a new patio slab. The storage room floor was also repaired. All of the fences were repaired and the landscaping was cleaned up.

The house was rented on January 1, 2012, for $700 a month with a $300 deposit. We had originally wanted $750, however, having a tenant move in right away was worth taking the $50 off the first year's rent to me. The rent will increase the second year to $750 a month.

The total cost with repairs was about $35,000. The annual income (at $750 per month rental) would be $9,000. Taxes were $1200 a year; insurance was $650. Net income on this property was $6650 a year. Property value, based on comparable listings (comps), was estimated to be $75,000, after the rehabilitation work was done. That gave us a 20 percent annual return, cash on cash.

We refinanced the house to take out $40,000 cash to do another house. The payments on this loan were approximately $334 a month. Our net cash flow was $2640 a year after refinancing. As we would have no cash in the deal after refinancing, the return was 100 percent a year, cash on cash.

Purchase: Midcrown Office Building

We found this office building for sale at $350,000. At that price it was a good deal, so we purchased it. This purchase, when fully rented, will be the equivalent of 20 front doors (assuming $250 a front door).

There was an office that had been a doctor's office (2200 sq. ft.), and three other suites that could be used by many other types of businesses.

The prior owners paid $450,000 and they put about $150,000 more into it.

Having closed their practice, the building sat empty for three years or so. Wire thieves broke in and the resulting damage further discouraged the owners, who finally lowered the asking price.

Description: Corner lot, glass storefront, 10-foot-wide covered walkway, tilt wall construction.

Size: 6583 square feet, pole sign, parking for 30-plus cars, four suites, separate electrical service.

Needed: New landscaping, trees trimmed, driveways and parking lot sealed and re-striped, handicapped signs, clean up and some repairs, new copper main lead wires in all suites, alarms, security cameras, some fence work for enhanced security, and the pole sign repainted. The cost estimate was $30,000.

Possible other improvements were adding a digital advertising sign (4'x8' or 6'x8' full color) as a leasing incentive.

The building should provide $10,000 to $14,000 per month in rental income at a monthly carrying cost of $5000, including all taxes and payments.

The building is on a 15-year amortization. The downpayment was provided at 12 percent interest on an interest-only note. Repairs will be paid in cash.

Appraised value was $500,000. The **estimated value** after being fully leased was $600,000-plus.

Marketing: Loop net, MLS, on-site banners, and advertising weekly in the San Antonio business newspaper. We held an open house when all was ready. Commission to agents could cost four percent of the lease amount for the whole lease term.

Commercial buildings have a different set of risk factors compared to residential properties. You need more money to buy, plus experience to market them. Carrying costs can be high and tenants can take longer to acquire but tend to stay in place longer.

Class B: Class B buildings are generally a little older, but still have good quality management and tenants. Oftentimes, value-added investors target these buildings as investments, since well-located Class B buildings can be returned to their Class A glory through renovation, such as facade and common area improvements. Class B buildings should generally not be functionally obsolete and should be well maintained.

Do not try this without experience and deep pockets. I have 20 years of experience with commercial property leasing. **Keep in mind, residential is easier and less risky for the inexperienced investor.**

This purchase fit our Gem Rental Properties business plan even though it was non-residential. We felt it was the right opportunity because of the free cash flow it could produce.

In a better lending environment and economy, this building would have sold for the $550,000 the previous owner had wanted.

After running the numbers, I estimated a **free cash flow** of $47,582.

Getting the Money to Expand

I am always looking for people who will lend me money on one of my properties. I give them a first lien on the real estate and pay the lender seven or eight percent interest– typically eight percent for amounts over $40,000, with a commitment of five years or longer. Payments can be monthly, quarterly, annually, or any way we agree.

I borrow no more than 60 percent of the value of the property, based on comps, or cash flow at a 10 percent cap rate. This is to protect the lender as well as assure that I have good positive cash flow.

The biggest mistake I see real estate investors make is to borrow too much money, leaving them with insufficient positive cash flows. I want to be able to withstand a 20 percent vacancy rate and still pay my lenders. (I have never had a vacancy rate above eight percent a year, but it could still happen in the days to come.)

The other reason to keep the percentage of borrowed funds low is to give me spendable income. This will allow me more money to invest from incoming rents, to maintain my properties sufficiently, thereby keeping the values up, and because I will sleep better knowing I can pay the bills. I suggest you do the same.

Getting started is harder than growing your enterprise. Making sure that growth makes financial sense takes discipline.

If you have not started your own investment adventure...*get with the program!*

How does this work?

I buy a house that needs rehabilitating, fix it up, and rent it out.

EXAMPLE

I buy a house for $60,000 that, once repaired and updated, would be worth $110,000. I spend $20,000 to rehabilitate the place. I rent it for $1100 a month. With a resale value of $110,000, I would refinance up to 60 percent of the $110,000, i.e., $66,000. That would yield me a mortgage payment of $484 a month, plus taxes and insurance of, say, $300 a month. That would leave me a positive cash flow of $316 a month for my efforts. The $66,000 I borrow should net me $65,000 after loan closing costs to use to buy another house.

In the above example, the private lender gets eight percent interest on their money (many times the current bank CD rate). I have $15,000 of my money in the deal, earning me $3700 a year. That is a 24 percent return on my money, assuming 100 percent occupancy. Even if I am vacant one month and have $600 in repairs, I still have $2000 left and a 14 percent return, cash on cash.

Why do I do this?

Not for the $300 a month, but rather for many times the $300 a month coming in. Multiply that by **ten, twenty,** or **fifty.** What's enough money coming in to keep you smiling?

My goal is 100 units, or front doors. With that kind of money, I can hire enough help that all I have to do is oversee the staff and search out new opportunities. And that is just from the cash flow.

Where is the rest of the money?

Real estate has historically gone up in value over time (appreciation). This will continue to be true, bubbles notwithstanding. Rents increase over time (inflation), thus increasing your free cash flow. The government likes real estate, so you can take depreciation against your taxes, but there are some limitations on this. Because you fixed up your property, it is worth more than it cost you out of pocket (sweat equity). If you never sell the properties, you never pay any taxes on the sweat equity, or appreciation. And if you do ever pay the taxes on your gains, it is at the long-term capital gains rate. Now, how good is that?

Benefits

You pay your lenders more than banks do. You improve neighborhoods. You recycle properties. You give people a better place to live. You help the economy. You get richer. You help to create jobs. And, you get to play Monopoly with real houses. How cool is that?

CHAPTER SEVENTEEN

THINK RICH

In the process of getting rich, you can't help but create jobs
for others.

This book, when taken as a whole and put into practice, will soon have you thinking rich. Rich people (somewhere in the neighborhood of three to five percent of the population) think differently from the rest of us.

Thinking rich is an awareness of the fact that, in every decision you make,

---
Getting rich is a process

---

every action you take, there are opportunities to improve your lot in life. Rich people, whether they realize it or not, instinctively consider their financial future in every decision they make. It is this thinking, this learning, this understanding process, along with their willingness to be proactive, that makes them richer.

How do they do this? People who get money from a financial windfall and do not learn how to think rich soon find themselves broke again. Think about those stories of lottery winners who end up destitute. The people who want to be rich, but do not learn how to think rich, never get rich.

Rich people have developed a sense or a way of thinking that is different from most other people. If you ask a rich person about this, they may look at you blankly. But, as you talk with them about their achievements and their investments, you soon discover that they do indeed "think rich." They habitually weight all their decisions to take their financial interests into consideration. This is what gives them the edge, the self-confidence and the fortitude, to make things happen. Thinking rich is seeing opportunity and seizing that opportunity to change one's position in life, to get rich (or richer), and hopefully make the world a little better in the process.

How Much Is "Rich?"

Money is relative. By that I mean that, if you have a million dollars, it may not seem like a lot, but if you are broke, a thousand dollars seems like a lot. So, let us define rich.

Rich is having enough money to do what you want, when you want.

For some people, having a million dollars is being rich. I can personally attest that most people who have a million dollars do not think of that as being rich. They probably started out thinking a million dollars was rich, but that is not what they ended up concluding. I doubt you will think a million dollars makes you rich when you make it to a million dollars of net worth either. You *can* make it, by the way, if you really want to— to being rich that is, or accumulating a net worth of a million dollars.

For me, being rich is never being broke; **it's having enough monthly income** to be able to control how I spend my time, to be able to provide a good living for my family, and to be able to afford a few investments to occupy my mind. For Bill Gates, I think it is safe to assume that being rich means similar things that I have listed for myself, plus being able to make a difference in the world through philanthropy.

Who are the rich people? They are the top 5 percent of the population along with another 10 or 15 percent who make up the semi-rich. They are the movers and shakers of the world. They make investments, create jobs, start businesses, and create things. They are out inventing, developing, discovering, giving, and lending, and they make things happen. Cumulatively, they are out there directly or indirectly, in countless little ways, changing the reality of tomorrow for all of us.

They can't help but change the world. In the process of making money, you will find yourself making things happen, and the more money you make, the more things move forward as that money is put to work by you or whomever you entrust your investments. You or your agents are putting that money to work with the intention of seeing it grow. This happens because it is in everyone's best interest for it to happen. Throughout all of recorded history, we have evidence of man's advancement. In that process, you have people getting rich.

It might as well be you.

Getting rich is a process. First, you have to want it so much that you put the effort into making "Thinking Rich" a habit. Then, you have to find what motivates you, for it is your personal motivation that will get you to put your plan into action, rather than just thinking and talking about making money. Finally, you must have determination because determination is what keeps you going when the negativity of naysayers and your own fears start to set in.

In 2012, CNN *Money* reported that a mere 14 percent of American workers felt prepared for retirement and another 38 percent somewhat confident, while *Fortune* magazine reported that, according to a study by the Employee Benefits Research Institute, fully 20 percent of workers anticipate they will never have saved sufficiently to be able to retire—*ever.*

It used to be that some 50 to 60 percent of people felt sure of reaching retirement age with a comfortable retirement income, largely because of automatic investment plans, such as Social Security, 401(k)s, IRAs, and various other retirement plans. The money is taken away and invested for most people before they get their hands on it and, thus, the time value of long-term investing gets them to a comfortable retirement in spite of themselves.

Rich people also do these things. But, as has been proved by the shrinking economy and slashing of pensions and raising of retirement ages, this is no longer enough. Rich people add to their retirement income yields from various investments and that takes them to the next level. That is where you want to be, at a level that is not only secure but *beyond* comfortable.

Thinking Rich Concepts

Primary concepts

There are three primary stumbling blocks that you must overcome before you can truly "think rich."

- Fear

- Procrastination

- Self-doubt

Fear

We all have a natural inclination to fear risk, however, we must put that fear into perspective. To overcome fear, we have to break the problem down into manageable parts and make some decisions. The first problem is that we tend to get very **emotional where our money is involved.** So, how do you reduce the emotional effect when making your investment decisions?

The rich people I know take the emotion out of decision making as much as possible by first separating their personal and investment accounts. If you treat each investment account as a business, as my family and I do, then you will find it is much easier to make business decisions with regard to that money.

Second, we have a natural **fear of the unknown.** To that I say, study, study, study. The more you know, the better equipped you will be to handle each situation as it comes along, and the less fear you will experience.

Last, we have **a real fear of losing our money.** To conquer this one, you just need to get a little perspective. If you do your homework, buy wisely, and insure yourself, you greatly reduce your risk. As I told you earlier, as soon as we discovered things weren't going to blow up in our faces, we gained a little perspective.

Procrastination

You must overcome the tendency to put things off until tomorrow. Making money is a process of figuring out what to do and then doing it. Most people work at making a living until they develop a career and start making enough money to cover their cost of living. Then they go into idle mode, doing just enough to get by. Most people set up an automatic employer-sponsored retirement plan or cross their fingers and hope that Social Security will be adequate to provide for their old age. They occasionally think about getting rich, but once the monthly living costs are covered, they keep putting off getting rich. They procrastinate.

Self-doubt

You must overcome all feelings of self-doubt, any thoughts that you are not as deserving as anyone else. You deserve to be rich! Now, start thinking that way. Realizing you are just as deserving as anyone else will get rid of one more of the roadblocks that stop people from getting rich.

You are deserving. You are smart enough and you can do it. Children born into wealthy families just assume that, when they become adults, they will live a life similar to their parents'. More important, all of their relatives and friends make that same assumption. Because everyone is on the same course, everyone does what they are supposed to do, and, sure enough, these children are now living the good life, too.

I was born into a poor family of twelve kids. I was nine before I knew most people made their sandwiches with two pieces of bread. One Saturday, my mother's sister came to visit and showed us home movies and slides of their recent vacation trips. They were mostly of national parks and big, distant cities. These people seemed awfully rich to this 10-year-old boy.

I thought about what I'd seen all that next week and came to the decision that these were my relatives; if they can be rich, so can I. I was just as deserving as anyone else, I realized. I never questioned myself again; I just decided that I would be rich, and that I deserved to be rich. At the time I had no clue how important that decision—that conscious commitment—was.

What happened was that I started substituting YES for no. "Yes, I can," "Why not me?" and "Sure I can!" It wasn't long before people started saying things like, "Go ask Jim. He's always up for anything." People started making assumptions about me because I acted quickly and decisively. To them, I appeared to lack doubt or hesitation. In reality, what I had was confidence in my abilities and a willingness to assume responsibility.

218

Because people assumed I would be successful at whatever I did, they helped me, and I was successful at most of the things I did. The funny thing is that this is exactly the edge that rich people have. You can, by your actions and attitude, accrue success and wealth, by "thinking rich."

We owe it to ourselves to learn to "think rich."

My advice to you is to choose one area of investing and buy a book on that subject and read it. Buy several. The more you learn about that area of investing, the more expert you will become.

Colleges use this methodology. What you learn in college, at least for the first two years, is primarily *how to learn.* You can take that college methodology of studying, outlining, and implementation, and implement your own "Get Rich" plan.

Learning to get rich is like being a college student. You begin the freshman year not sure of what you want to do with the rest of your life or what you want to be. Maybe you're just a little unsure of your abilities. Four years later, you likely feel much more confident and ready to tackle the world. The professors only drilled and offered you encouragement, but you and the other students also taught yourselves and each other. You learned to think and respect each other's conclusions.

Do that with money and you are "thinking rich."

Learn to Think Rich

Thinking rich is the way rich people get rich and how they stay rich. Thinking rich is taking your current and your future financial position into account as you make countless little decisions throughout your everyday life. We are talking about changing the very way you think, the way you consider things, the way you analyze situations, the way you respond to events, the way you think about money, the way you interact with others concerning money.

I use the word money a lot, but I'm talking about any tool—anything that you own or control that has value or can increase your assets, including, but not limited to, your time, earning power, money, assets with a monetary value, property, education, and so on.

Almost every decision you make has the potential to add to (or subtract from) your wealth or affect it in some way. You need to make a habit of taking your wealth into consideration in every decision you make. Once you have done that, it is a small step toward thinking to maximize your wealth on a regular basis. The rewards for acquiring these habits are a wonderful, life-changing way of living for you and everyone around you.

"Think Rich" signs

In the beginning, I was trying to get rich, but everyday life was distracting, and I would forget to think about getting rich for days at a time. To solve this problem, I posted "Think Rich" signs everywhere to remind me to think about making money every day. Fellow workers, family members, and friends made fun of me for having signs in my car, on my phone at work, on my bedroom mirror and many other places—but it worked.

After about two years of working at thinking rich, it had become a habit, and I no longer needed the reminders. I replaced the "Think Rich" signs with "Think Positively."

EXAMPLE

A young man about to enter college asked his grandmother, who was of comfortable means, to help him to buy a car. Nothing expensive, he assured her, maybe a grand or two. She could easily have just written him a check and called it a day. Instead, she bought a car from an elderly friend of hers for $1200, transferred the title to her grandson, and had him sign a contract for the purchase price and related costs. In exchange, he agreed to mow her grass and do handyman work one afternoon a week at 10 dollars per hour, until the debt was repaid.

The young man gets a car. He has no obligation to repay the $1200 in cash, which he doesn't have. She gets her yardwork and other chores done, which is hard to find people to do at a reasonable cost. The young man learns responsibility and a life lesson. She gets to see her teenage grandson on a regular basis. And, most important, the whole family learns that, if you want something from Grandma, you must offer something in return.

This real life example illustrates how any event can be turned into a wealth-building or wealth-conserving one. Take this one small event and multiply it over this woman's lifetime and you get thousands of similar decisions that she has made that have resulted in her having a very comfortable lifestyle.

Thinking rich means looking for solutions

You must learn to approach each and every decision with your financial well-being as a key consideration. Most people do not make this consideration; they react to a situation or they look for an easy out or they make a decision because it feels good or is expected of them. As a result, most of the outcomes are less than optimal. Thinking rich means looking for the solutions or opportunities that give you the best possible outcomes. Over time, the habit of making optimized decisions makes you richer.

I have made it a habit of always saying, "Let me give this some thought, and I will get back to you," and I give them a specific day to expect my decision. I do my research and come up with the plan most beneficial to everyone involved. I respond to the other party in a timely fashion. Doing it this way, I get time for contemplation and the end result is often better because it is better thought out. Everyone who deals with me learns that it is best to have their act together when they approach me. They also find out that I do not jump through hoops because they failed to plan or procrastinated.

This method has another very important benefit: you gain respect. This respect accrues to you from relatives and strangers alike, from everyone with whom you do business.

The reason you get their respect is that you are asking questions in a calm, logical, nonjudgmental manner, rather than reacting without taking the necessary time for proper consideration and you get back to them with a well thought out plan or solution. If you do this consistently, people will learn that you are one to come to for solid solutions, not quick fixes. They will soon learn to save you for the important things, and not waste your time with the mundane, saving you time and grief in the process.

All of this makes you different from everyone else in their world, and that gains you respect. Plus, you are teaching them by example, as well as training them how you want to be treated. You get all of this just from making "thinking rich" a habit.

EXAMPLE

A man has a $70,000 lot he purchased, on which he intends to build a home. He is paying $700 a month on the note. He decides against building the house, so he lists the property for sale with a realtor. Not a single one of his decisions was made by "thinking rich." Let me explain.

First, the lot should not have been purchased until he was ready to build. If he wanted to tie up a particular lot, it should have been by way of an option or a cash purchase. The interest rate on the note is too high, and he is now paying taxes and to maintain it.

He listed the lot for sale and waited. When he told me about this land deal, I made the following "Think Rich" suggestions:

- he post a "for sale by owner" sign on it with his phone number; and

- list it for sale on Craigslist and in the local weekly newspaper.

He needs to get out from under the payments as soon as possible. Depending on a realtor to do this for him is foolhardy. A number of people prefer to call a "for sale by owner" number before a real estate agency. I pointed out that, since he is the one with the vested interest in selling his lot and because this was the only property he was focused on selling, he would return any potential buyer's calls faster. The realtor wants to sell prospective customers something, but it may not be *his* something.

I also suggested he try and renegotiate an interest-only payment deal with the bank. A further suggestion was that he talk to the original landowner about a "walk away clean" deal because the original land owner most likely has a guarantee on the loan to the bank. Also, he should talk with the bank about a "take over payment" deal for any buyer who did materialize, and ask the banker for any other suggestions on cutting his losses.

What the man in this example had done to get out of a bad deal was what most people would do—relinquish responsibility and hand it off to someone else to fix. What I did was to apply the "Think Rich" process to the same problem. If he implements my suggestions, he stands a better chance of reducing his losses, which is the same as making more money because it improves his current cash flow.

EXAMPLE

One day I drove past a billboard advertising new homes. I had an idea. I started calling billboard companies and asked if they had a new site locater department. I soon learned which company was the big dog in town and informed them I had a great location for a sign.

They asked a lot of questions that sent me off to take photos and contact the highway department to obtain traffic counts. I sent them the requested information and, a few weeks later, they sent out an acquisition representative. Soon thereafter, I had a lease at $695 a month on property I already owned. There were plenty of other landowners around me who could have done the same thing I did, but they didn't. I was the only one "thinking rich." When I sold that property four years later, I was able to add $60,000 to the price for the value of that billboard lease. I made $93,000, before taxes, on one deal from "thinking rich."

Get started

Let's talk about those "Think Rich" signs another minute. Go buy a pack of Post-it® notes and get started. Put them everywhere you will see them regularly, multiple times a day. Forty years later, I still have my notes up. I use one as a bookmark; there are seven on my desk, one over my truck's tachometer, and one on my computer. Get started and, a little at a time, you will get there.

Opportunities are everywhere

Opportunities happen every day

Every time you hear of something happening or see something occur, ask yourself the question: "How can someone make money from that?" Almost everything that happens is an opportunity to make money.

If you do this long enough, it becomes a way of thinking, a habit.

EXAMPLE

Let's say you hear a news report that Amazon is coming out with an electronic book reader. A few weeks later, you hear another company will have one out by Christmas. You assume that, with all this free publicity, electronic book readers will be a hot Christmas item. You buy a thousand shares of Amazon in November.

In December, Amazon announces that the reader is the hottest item this year. **Was that a predictable press release, or what?** Amazon stock goes up and you sell fast or put in a stop loss order to protect your profit. That is "thinking rich" put into action.

EXAMPLE

The stock market hit a low in February 2009. For months, the stock market decline had been in the news; people were beginning to speculate on where the bottom was. Newscasters were spouting about how much everyone had lost on the way down. The news was doom and gloom, but just maybe there was some light ahead.

Mutual fund withdrawals had slowed down. I asked myself, "Where is all of that 401(k) money still being deducted from millions of people's paychecks going? The money was still out there, so where was it being invested? Based on historical investing and the alternatives out there, the only long-term option was stocks. The question now was *When?*

I put $18,000 (all the cash I had at the time) in the stock market and made $20,000 on it in four months. That was "thinking rich" in action.

At the end of 2009, real estate prices had been down for over a year and people were starting to talk about having hit the bottom. I was putting in offers on bargain-priced apartments intending to buy up all I could get that were possible to finance. Why? Because people always need a place to live and housing has shelter value. The prices, I knew, would inevitably start to rise again in a few years and I wanted to make another chunk of change from what I knew would happen. Some parts of the future are predictable.

There is opportunity around you every day. Open your eyes and see; open your ears and listen; open your mind and think. The questions are these: "How might anyone benefit from this?" "Why shouldn't it be me?" Ask these questions long enough, often enough, and you will be "thinking rich."

EXAMPLE

I was asked by my nephew to go along with him as he shopped for a manufactured (prefabricated) house. I was sitting in the lobby of the sales center waiting for him when a woman came in, wanting to sell her mobile home. The manager shook his head and said they were not interested. I followed her out and got her phone number.

The next week I purchased her used mobile home.

What if $100,000 came your way?

Let us suppose for a minute that you had $100,000 cash in the bank. What would you do? What would your thought processes be? Not so easy, is it? What would a "**Think Rich**" person do with the same amount?

If you are a "**Think Rich**" person, you have your house in order. You live within your means, and you have a plan for your financial future. It is that plan that will provide you with a starting place for your thought process. Let us walk through the thought process, a series of questions targeted toward the highest and best use of the funds.

- What are the tax consequences of this money?

- Is the money parked in an interest-bearing account?

- Where could I invest this money to get the highest rate of return?

- Should I look for long- or short-term investments?

- What is the current direction of interest rates?

- What else could I do with it to increase my yearly cash income long term?

- Do I have the time or skills for an active investment or should I seek a passive investment?

- How will this money affect or change my "get rich" plan?

- Do I have the needed skills for the intended use or do I need assistance?

You answered some key questions when you made your "Get Rich" plan:

- Do I like passive vs. active investments?

- How much risk am I willing to assume?

- What is a good rate of return for me?

- What types of investments interest me?

- What are the returns on various investment options?

- Do I have an emergency fund?

Most people who get a large sum of money and who do not have a plan generally are broke within six months of getting the money. This happens because they were not prepared and lacked the financial management skills to do otherwise. Most people think of money as necessary to survive and they know they are supposed to save some for when they get old. What they should have been taught is that money is also a tool that can make them more money. They need only to learn to use this tool. To do that, they must change the way they think about money.

Money is a tool

The rich get richer partially because they have money working for them every day, but mostly because they consider the highest and best use of the money that comes their way. We all make money mistakes; we all look back and say we should have done this or that instead. I am guilty of making bad decisions about money every week, but I know that I only have to get it right half of the time to get ahead. The other thing I know is that, in order to get it right half of the time, I have to work at it.

My advice to anyone deciding what to do with a large sum of money is to park it in a money market account and take your time making decisions. If you do nothing for six months but plan and research your options, then you have done the right thing.

Money is a tool

Money is nothing more than a tool. At first blush, you would not think this is a profound statement, but it is. Once it really hits you, it will be a revelation. That is because you will then be able to separate feelings and anxieties from your money decisions.

Most people associate money with their personal worth, with what others think about them. They mix up how they feel about their job with how much they get paid for doing that job. They value other people by how much money they make, or by how much money they contribute.

They value money for what it can buy them, and how they feel about that is how they feel about money. They worry about money or the lack thereof. They fight over money. Yet, they do not have a household budget or a plan for making or spending the very thing that consumes so much of their time and energy.

Money is a tool which, when properly used, provides you with the necessities of life and with a standard of living based on your ability to acquire it. That is it—nothing more.

Anything else you attribute to money is a value that you have decided to give it, for whatever selfish or silly reasons that your mind has conjured up. Sounds awful, doesn't it?

I think we can agree that a pencil is quite a useful tool. Think of all the things you can do with a pencil. What could a trained artist do with that pencil? What about a writer? A lawmaker? Or a CPA or, God forbid, an IRS auditor? What about someone intending to do you harm? Your view of a simple pencil has now altered—it has become a tool with unlimited potential.

Money is a tool, a tool you must learn how to use in various ways. It is well worth the time you will need to put into learning to use money for its highest and best use, to make your life whatever you want it to be. **Thinking rich is doing just that.**

If you were lucky, you were born into a family that understood basic economic concepts and they assisted you in getting the necessary education and life skills to make a living. Again, if you were lucky, you didn't get into a big financial mess before you figured it out. From this point, you have to learn budgeting, management, investing, risk management and self-control. I know, these are business concepts, but **it is your life's business.**

Some things NOT to do

Do not argue about money; it's a total waste of time. Your time can be better spent making more money to fix the underlying problem.

Do not associate with people who continually undermine your money plans.

Do not spend more than you can afford.

Do not lend money you cannot afford to donate.

Do not get emotional about a money issue. When you do, you cannot think rationally to solve the issue that caused the emotions to spike. Look at the problem, not the symptoms.

Some things TO do

Have a money plan. Do it anyway, on paper preferably. Call it a budget, or a future money plan, if you will. By the time you have done your tenth draft, it will start to make sense. Your money plan will be constantly evolving. You can almost always trace people's money problems to a failure to plan, or a failure to implement the plan.

Fill out a financial statement once a year. It is a good road map that will improve your money management skills over the years.

Work toward getting multiple sources of income. It's about not putting all your eggs in one basket. It is amazing how much freedom you will have with money coming in from several sources. **For example,** you could have money from salary, from other household earners, from rents, from investments, from notes receivable, from odd jobs, from garage sales, from a part-time business, and so on. Every rich person I know has multiple sources of income.

Always be looking for ways to increase your household income. That is what "thinking rich" is about, improving your standard of living.

Protect your assets by planning for negative possibilities. You cannot insure against every contingency, but reasonable planning should be done. You should have at least basic health insurance, as well as fire and hazard, liability, and life insurance. Insurance for other types of hazards that might wreak varying degrees of havoc with the best-laid plans are a matter of choice and should be considered within a cost-benefit analysis.

Keep in mind that money is but a tool. When you reach a point where you can say, "It's just money; I can always earn more," you will quit worrying and you will be "thinking rich." After all, "life, liberty, and the pursuit of happiness" are the true measures of wealth.

CHAPTER EIGHTEEN

REAL ESTATE Q&A

Q: How much should I charge for rent?

A: A simple rule of thumb formula is to take the purchase price of the house (or unit) and divide it by 100. If a house costs you $100,000, then the rent should be about $1000 a month.

Having said that, you need to know what similar properties are renting for in your area. About every six months, it pays to look at a few similar properties to determine the current rental rates and adjust your rents accordingly. The prevailing rental rate information is critical when you are looking to buy because it will help you establish the maximum price that you are willing to pay.

This website will help you determine the rental rates in your area: http://www.rentrange.com/

Q: How much should I improve a property?

A: Enough to attract tenants. When you look at other properties to buy (or get a feel for the rental rates), look at the condition and amenities being offered, as they will serve as a guide for your own properties. I only improve a property enough to attract rents in a given price range. When I show a property and the potential renters are leaving, I ask them what they would have liked to see different or what they did not like. See if you can ask them a few questions. Do not over-improve your property, but don't be a cheapskate either.

Q: How do I know a good deal when I see it?

A: If you do your homework, you will know it when it presents itself. Reading this book will add to your knowledge and will help you to spot great deals. My general rule of thumb when considering a property for purchase is that it must have a 15 percent-plus cap rate, its expenses must not exceed 50 percent of the rent collected, and its asking price must be less than 10 times the annual net income. I particularly like properties that I know are being rented too cheaply.

Q: How do I find good deals?

A: Look, look, and then look some more. Tell everyone—and I mean *everyone*—that you are looking for real estate to buy, and pass out your phone number and email address liberally. It may well take six months of broadcasting that you are looking, but a deal will eventually come your way if you persist.

Look at REO websites, check newspaper ads, and drive the streets. Always be on the lookout for properties. One hundred properties later, you just might find that deal. If not, start on the second hundred. Deals are out there, millions of them, so look, always and often.

Don't forget to check out sites like Craigslist, read the classified ads, and tell your entire network of friends and acquaintances.

Q: How do I get the money?

A: Any way you can. Throughout this book, I reveal ways to get the money and reduce the amount of money needed, plus information on financing. Money is nothing more than a tool and everyone who has it needs it to be working. So, the money is there for you to find. You might want to look at sites like personalrealestateinvestormag.com for additional sources.

Relatives are another great source for loans. As you are telling everyone you are looking for properties, some will ask about the business and may want to participate by lending you money. You can also find partners. Be creative. You have access to more money than you think.

Q: How do I overcome the initial fear? I've got butterflies the size of bats!

A: This is a hard one. You just have to do your first deal. I did my first deal (a duplex) with a realtor holding my hand through the process. I did not make much money on that first deal and I sold it a year later, breaking even on price. But I needed to get that first deal behind me in order to build my confidence.

My next two deals involved seller-carried notes and were very profitable. I still make money on one of them today, 30 years later. Find a small property that will rent for at least enough to cover the note and *just do it*. When you discover that the world hasn't come to an end, your butterflies will begin to fly away.

Q: Why don't more people do real estate investing if it's so great?

A: Fear. Fear of loss, lack of money, fear the renters will tear things up, and on and on. Lack of know-how lies at the root of all the fear and misunderstanding concerning what being a landlord is like. Just remember, someone owns all those rental houses and apartments out there. There are more landlords than you can imagine.

Q: How do I avoid bad tenants?

A: Most of the behavior that makes for a bad tenant is avoidable if you screen your tenants carefully. Charge an application fee of, say, $45, enough to cover the costs of a background check, and then pay to have it done, something which can also be online. Call the potential renter's past landlord(s) and their job reference. That should help you avoid most of the problems. Ask for a security deposit. If the tenant cannot manage a security deposit on top of the rent, then it's a reasonable bet that they're too much of a risk—that they'll have difficulty coming up with their monthly rent on a regular basis.

Q: What if the renters do significant damage?

A: Despite your best efforts, you may eventually run across a bad tenant. Let's put the damages into perspective. What is the worst that can happen? Stolen appliances? Holes in the walls? It has been my experience that all of this damage might cost about $3,000 to fix, and rarely does it cost $5,000 (only once in my 35 years). The average undesirable tenant costs a landlord about $1,500, including eviction costs. Set aside $3,000 of your cash flow in a savings account and you will sleep better.

Most every time I have had this happen, after fixing a ruined apartment, I have been able to raise the rent by another $25 to $50 a month and quickly recouped my loss.

Q: I have two rental houses, but they barely make any money. What should I do?

A: By this, you probably mean they have very little cash flow beyond their expenses. I have had several of these over the years and loved them all. One I kept until it was fully paid for by the rental income; at that point, the rent paid to me was all profit. Also, you still make some money, assuming you are raising the rents every year (about four percent) to cover repairs and tax increases, etc. Don't forget that you make money from the value of the property appreciating, that you save money in taxes when you depreciate the property, and that you get a little richer each month as your equity increases. Long term, you win!

Q: What are the average returns on real estate investing?

A: This depends on a number of factors and varies widely. Having said that, you can expect about 12 percent if you pay cash for the properties. The total returns from all the ways the property makes you money can be as much as 15 to 20 percent per year. If you use some leverage, or if you find ways to add value, the returns can easily beat 12 percent.

Q: I have not had much luck with real estate agents. What is your take on them?

A: In my experience, maybe one in 100 agents adds any real value. Most are too concerned with their commissions to serve either the buyer or the seller well. They sometimes get in the way of a deal getting done.

Those agents who are the top producers and close the most deals do not worry about commissions; they just do deals. These are the agents I like. They let the paycheck take care of itself. A good agent takes care of you, the buyer, because that serves the seller best. Those agents failing to understand that the buyer is important leave the trade when the market turns downward and the going gets tough. Good agents can be found. If you are always looking for deals, you will cross paths with quality agents.

Q: Why do I find it so hard to get started as an investor?

A: Because there is never enough money and you have a lot to learn. Then, there is figuring out where to start. Start by reading all the sections of this book. Then, just do that first deal to get your feet wet.

As for the fear factor, just keep in mind that the risk is only the difference between what you pay for the property and what you sell it for, if things do not work out. The risk is perhaps a few thousand dollars, and, let's be honest, you risk that much when you buy a new car—the only difference is that you are guaranteed to suffer a loss in value with a new car, but not in real estate.

As for getting loans, it is a matter of filling out loan requests until someone says yes. I was once turned down 13 times before I was approved at 10 percent down. But I got the loan.

The biggest obstacle to getting rich in any endeavor is the person looking back at you in the mirror.

Q: How much interest should I expect to pay?
A: As little as you can manage to negotiate.

Here's a formula I use. Calculate the annual net operating income of a property by subtracting all the property expenses, from taxes and insurance to utilities and any maintenance, from the gross rental (operating) income. Divide that net income by the purchase price and multiply by 100 to get the net income percent figure.

If the interest rate you're offered is less than three-quarters of that property's net income percent, then take the deal.

For example, if a property's net annual income is $12,000 and the purchase price is $100,000, dividing 12,000 by 100,000 and then multiplying by 100 will give you 12. Three-quarters of 12 equals 9. Therefore a loan at 7, 8 or 9 percent is viable—the lower the interest rate, the higher the positive cash flow.

Another way to look at loans is that the loan payments should come to 75 percent or less of the net cash flow, or 50 percent or less of the gross rents.

Appendix A

LETTER TO POTENTIAL INVESTORS

10 Northeast Parkway
San Antonio, TX 78218
Tel: 210-555-2222
Fax 210-555-3333
E-mail: jglasgow@browser.com

Investor's Name
Street Address
City, State, Zip

A SELF-STORAGE INVESTMENT OPPORTUNITY

Dear Investor:

I am writing to you to acquaint you with an investment opportunity in a limited partnership, to be known as L410E/ Rigsby Self-Storage LP, which will develop a self-storage facility on the east side of San Antonio, Texas.

Since the start of the self-storage industry in the early 1970s, the self-storage business has grown into one of the most profitable real estate-based businesses. A mature self-storage property can generate cash-on-cash returns approaching 18 percent annually.

In my opinion, an investment in the securities of L410E/Rigsby Self-Storage LP can be considered a conservative business risk, and a rare opportunity to join other investors to develop a profitable self-storage facility. As General Partner, I am of the opinion that the minimum return (on capital invested) over five years will be 75 percent, and the maximum total return upon sale of the property could be as high as 150 percent.

Jim Glasgow as General Partner

I will act as General Partner. For the past 25 years, I have been in the portable storage building business and, during that time, I monitored the self-storage industry as a competitor. For the past two years, I have researched the self-storage industry with the intent to develop a facility, and commissioned an independent feasibility study to determine the feasibility of constructing a facility on the east side of San Antonio. With that study's positive indication for the profitable development of a self-storage property, I have decided to proceed with development. I have chosen a Limited Partnership as the best method to raise the necessary equity capital.

My Personal Investment

In addition to acting as General Partner, I will also be participating as a limited partner with an equity investment of $200,000.

75–150 Percent Profit Potential

Each Limited Partner will receive an accrued preferred simple interest of eight (8) percent annually on the capital invested. After payment of debt service and payment to the partners of accrued preferred interest, the Limited Partners will receive 50 percent of the quarterly net operating profits. Upon the sale of the facility, the investors will receive from the net sales proceeds, after settlement of any outstanding partnership obligations, their initial capital investment coupled with any accrued interest due to their account, followed by 50 percent of the remaining sale profits.

As General Partner, I am of the opinion that the minimum expected return to investors should be 75 percent over five (5) years, with the potential total return as high as 150 percent of the invested capital.

Investment Units Being Offered

Twenty-five (25) investment units are being sold at $20,000 per unit to raise $500,000 in equity. Approximately 50 percent of units have been pledged to other investors. The balance of the property and development costs will be borrowed funds, with the note being signed by the General Partner.

This letter is not an offer to sell securities; the offer is made only in the offering prospectus.

Risk and Taxes

All investments contain risk and you may want to consult your CPA or other adviser as to the suitability of this investment for your individual situation. It is my understanding that losses from depreciation can only be used to offset profits from other passive investments, that distributions from limited partnership profits are considered passive income, and that profits upon the sale of the facility will be treated as long-term capital gains.

Inquiries

In the event that you have interest and would like to discuss the investment opportunity further, I would be pleased to meet with you to review the feasibility study, limited partnership agreement, subscription agreement, prospectus, and any other pertinent documents in order to answer any questions you may have. Please contact me to discuss or arrange a meeting, either at my office or other location you prefer.

The Next Step
If you feel this investment might be right for you, please call me for a copy of the Limited Partnership Agreement. The sale of partnership/ investment units will close on September 15, 2004, or when all twenty-five (25) units are sold, whichever is earliest.

Once you have read the Limited Partnership Agreement and agree to invest, sign both the Subscription Agreement and Partnership Agreement and forward the originals to my attention with a check for the total number of units desired ($20,000 per unit) or a note indicating the date you intend to make payment.

Once your subscription is accepted, you will receive an Affidavit of Payment of Capital along with executed copies of the agreements. When the Partnership's application is filed with the state, you will receive a Certificate of Partnership.

I look forward to a mutually rewarding investment experience with you.

Sincerely yours,
Jim E. Glasgow Sr.

References available upon request
Enclosures:
Prospectus
Subscription agreement
Résumé
Referral fax

Appendix B

SAMPLE PROSPECTUS

L410E/Rigsby Self-Storage LP
10 Northeast Parkway
San Antonio, TX 78218
Tel: 210-555-2222
Fax: 210-555-3333
E-mail: jglasgow@browser.com

Investment Units Offered

Twenty-five (25) investment units (heretofore referred to as "Units") in L410E/Rigsby Self-Storage, LP, a Texas limited partnership (heretofore referred to as "The Partnership"), with James E. Glasgow Sr. acting as general partner (heretofore referred to as "General Partner"), to be formed for the purpose of acquiring, developing, owning, renting, maintaining, and/or holding as an investment, a self-storage facility of at least 45,000 square feet to be constructed on property fronting Loop 410 East, in San Antonio, Texas.

Price Per Limited Partnership Investment Unit: $20,000

Sales commission: None

Total Subscription: $500,000

This limited partnership shall begin the day the Certificate of the Limited Partnership is duly filed, and shall continue for seven years, until September 15, 2011, at which time it shall terminate in accordance with the Limited Partnership Agreement.

Appropriateness of Investment

These units should be purchased only as long-term investments. Units are not freely transferable. No market exists for the units or is expected to develop in the future. Premature sale of these securities is not advised.

Terms of Offering

Minimum subscription: $20,000 per unit, cash on or before September 15, 2004. The General Partner reserves the right to make the final determination regarding the issuance of all units. This offering will terminate on or before September 15, 2004 (extendable up to 60 days).

The General Partner shall hold subscription proceeds in trust via an escrow account until the Partnership is activated. In the event that a minimum of $400,000 is not subscribed, the General Partner shall have the option to purchase the remaining Units of the Partnership for his own account, with the right to resell same; or, the General Partner may terminate the offering and return the invested money to the subscribers without interest.

Return to Limited Partner

Each partner shall have a capital account maintained on the books of the Partnership that includes invested capital plus eight (8) percent preferred simple accrued interest, minus the partner's allocations of net loss and share of distributions. Net income and net loss shall be allocated as follows:

a. Net operating income after payment of mortgage note or note interest (NOI) shall be first applied toward the limited partners' eight (8) percent preferred simple accrued interest on their capital contributions.

b. Secondly, any monthly NOI in excess of payment of item (a) above will be distributed as follows: 50 percent to the general partners and 50 percent to the limited partners, to be shared among them in accordance with each limited partner's prorated share of capital contribution.

c. Upon dissolution of the Partnership, the capital account of the partners shall be returned.

Upon sale of Partnership assets, the net proceeds will be distributed in the following order:

a. First, to pay off all mortgages, debts, and outstanding expenses of the Partnership.

b. Second, to pay any expenses related to the disposal of the Partnerships assets and dissolution of the Partnership.

c. Third, return of the limited partners' original capital investment.

d. Fourth, payment of any fees due General Partner under this agreement.

e. Fifth, payment of any interest owed to the limited partners.

f. Finally, division of the balance of the proceeds and any reserve account balance equally between the General Partner (50 percent) and the limited partners (50 percent), to be shared among them based on their prorated capital contributions.

Refinancing

Upon refinancing for other than facility expansion of the Partnership's assets, the net proceeds after cost of refinancing will be distributed in the following order:

a. First, payment of any accrued interest owed to the limited partners.

b. Second, the return of the partners' original capital contributions.

c. Third, payment of any fees due the General Partner under this agreement.

d. Fourth, division of the balance of the proceeds equally between the General Partner (50 percent) and the limited partners (50 percent), to be shared among them based on their prorated capital contributions.

Further Assessments

Further assessments are possible but not contemplated.

Distribution

Distribution and sale of units will only be made through James E. Glasgow Sr, G.P., 10 Northeast Parkway, San Antonio, TX 78218 Tel: 210-555-2222, Fax: 210-555-3333 Email: jglasgow@browser.com

Depreciation Method

The General Partner shall have the right to select the depreciation method most suitable to Partnership objectives. It is probable that the Partnership will use component depreciation to the extent allowable to accelerate depreciation.

Leverage

The acquisition of the Partnership property and development of improvements will be on a 70–75 percent loan to a 30–25 percent equity basis. The General Partner will sign the note(s).

The General Partner may elect to finance the Partnership's assets during the term of the Partnership to construct phase two or to return a portion of the limited partner's contribution to each partner. The use of financing "leverage" could/would increase the rate of return on capital invested.

Location

The L410E/Rigsby Self-Storage facility will be located between Hwy 10 East and Hwy 87 (Rigsby) along Loop 410E on the west side of the highway.

Feasibility Study

A self-storage market analysis and feasibility study was completed in October 2003, which showed:

- Total estimated demand at 45,000 square feet (SF)

- Recommended climate-controlled space at 20–25% of the proposed space

- Estimated rent at $8.24/SF

- Estimated expenses at $2.95/SF

- Estimated stabilized net operating income (NOI) at $4.40/SF, excluding debt service

- Estimated lease-up in 14–16 months

- Estimated facility cost at $1,700,000, including land cost

General Market Overview

The subject is a proposed self-storage facility. General parameters in the industry indicate that a majority of the demand for these facilities will come from a three-mile radius. The location of the subject site does not present any major barriers within this radius and demand is based on a majority of the customers coming from the three-mile radius.

Population figures for the three-mile radius are provided by National Decision Systems as of September 3, 2003, and are based on the 2000 Census figures, adjusted to 2003.

According to National Decision Systems, population growth is estimated to average approximately 0.9 percent per year over the next five (5) years for the three-mile radius. National Decision Systems projects the three-mile radius population to be 41,296 in 2008.

The parameters of the subject sites are well located and, as such, should have the physical characteristics considered excellent for a potential self-storage development. The proposed location has good visibility along a well-traveled major thoroughfare. Assuming that the proposed project is well designed, well built, priced competitively, includes amenities similar to the competition in the market, and consists of the proper unit mix, the project is expected to capture more than its fair market share.

The complete 38-page feasibility study is available for review upon request.

Construction Costs

Estimated land size: 2.4 acres
Estimated net rentable square footage: 45,000
Estimated cost of construction: $1,427,619
Estimated land cost: $504,000
Total cost estimate: $1,827,619
Estimated loan amount: $1,300,000

Compensation and Fees

The fees shown below were not determined by arm's length negotiation.

For services as General Partner, for providing partnership management services, and assuming all risks and liabilities involved in the acquisition and management of such a project, the General Partner and affiliates are to be paid the following fees, profits, reimbursements, and shares of distribution set forth below.

The General Partner shall be entitled to a monthly payment of one (1) percent of the gross income to be designated as an asset management fee.

Any monthly NOI, after note payments and the bringing of the limited partners' accrued preferred interest payments and reserve account current, will be split evenly between the General Partner (50 percent) and the limited partners (50 percent).

The General Partner shall be entitled to a developer's fee of $100,000.00, to be taken as limited partnership shares for a total of five (5) Units.

Upon refinancing of the Partnership's assets, the net proceeds, after costs of refinancing and payment of any accrued preferred interest owed to the limited partners, the return of the limited partners' original capital contributions, and the payment of any fees due the General Partner under the limited partnership agreement, the balance of the proceeds will be divided equally between the General Partner (50 percent) and the limited partners (50 percent), to be shared among them based on their prorated capital contributions.

Upon the sale of Partnership's assets, the balance of the proceeds and any reserve account balance after payments to limited partners as outlined in the Return to Limited Partner clause above, will be divided equally between the General Partner (50 percent) and the limited partners (50 percent), to be shared among them based on their prorated capital contributions.

The General Partner shall receive two (2) percent of the sales price as a disposition fee.

Dissolution and Termination

The Partnership is for a minimum term of three (3) years or a maximum term of seven (7) years, at which time the Partnership's assets are to be sold and the proceeds distributed as per the terms of the Partnership Agreement.

The General Partner may sell the Partnership's assets and terminate the Partnership when, in the General Partner's judgment, it is in the best interest of the Partnership to do so. Proceeds of a sale will be distributed according to the terms of the Partnership Agreement.

Life Insurance

Life insurance will be maintained on the General Partner, made payable to the Partnership in the amount of $500,000, such proceeds to be used to reduce any of the Partnership's outstanding mortgages, with any excess to be used for the return of invested capital to the limited investors.

Management of the Self-storage Facility

Daily management of the self-storage facility will be contracted to a professional management company specializing in the self-storage industry.

Documents

Copies of the Limited Partnership Agreement, feasibility study, and other related documents are available at the office of the General Partner.

Pro Forma Financial Projections*

*Phase One only

	Year 1	Year 2	Year 3	Year 4	Year 5
Income	117,993	323,012	351,432	360,217	369,223
Expenses	122,460	125,297	148,258	152,215	156,270
NOI	4,467	149,264	203,173	208,003	212,953
ROI	<16%>	11%	22%	23%	24%
Payments	78,000	93,000	93,000	93,000	93,000

Lease-up losses
Year 1: ($20,822)
Year 2: ($48,452)

Return is estimated based on a total investment capital account of $500,000.

A sales price based on a nine (9) percent cap rate would be $2,350,000 for a pro forma profit on the sale of the facility of approximately $550,000.

A total return over five (5) years of 115 percent of capital invested can be expected.

Risk
The General Partner has taken and will continue to take every reasonable precaution to mitigate the risk as much as possible. It is the belief of the General Partner that the estimates used in preparing the Pro Forma are conservative; and that, with construction of a Phase Two to increase the available square footage for rent, the performance can be enhanced.

Some Potential Risks
• Land unacquirable for the estimated price

251

- Debt service interest rate is higher than seven (7) percent

- A competitor opens up before we reach 80 percent occupancy

- A sale cannot be consummated at the time or price anticipated

Conclusion

In the opinion of the General Partner, an investment in the securities of L410E Rigsby Self-Storage LP can be considered a conservative business risk and a rare opportunity to join other investors to develop a self-storage facility. The General Partner is of the opinion that the minimum return (on capital invested) over five (5) years will be 75 percent, and the maximum return could be as high as 150 percent over five (5) years.

In the opinion of the General Partner, the feasibility study has underrated the market demand and the area's growth rate. Our research tells us that early losses from depreciation can only be used to offset other passive income and that long-term profits paid to Limited Partners will be taxed at capital gains rates. It is advisable that any investor consult with the appropriate accountant or other tax advisor.

The enclosed Subscription Agreement can be used to apply for shares in this investment.

Appendix C

SAMPLE SUBSCRIPTION TO LIMITED PARTNER UNITS

To: L410E/Rigsby LP
10 Northeast Parkway
San Antonio, TX 78218
Tel: 210-555-2222
Fax: 210-555-3333
E-mail: L410E_RigsbyLP@browser.com

The undersigned tenders this subscription, together with payment of the purchase price of $20,000 per unit, for ____ unit(s) in L410E/Rigsby LP, a limited partnership organized under the Uniform Limited Partnership Act of the state of Texas, being offered by the offering Prospectus dated June 15, 2004 (heretofore known as the "offering circular"). It is understood that the amount payable for each unit tendered is to be deposited in escrow with _____ Bank for the benefit of the undersigned and will be returned promptly in the event that a minimum of 20 units offered by the offering circular are not subscribed and paid for by September 15, 2004.

The undersigned represents and warrants that he/she is a resident of the state of Texas and either (i) has a net worth (excluding, for this purpose, the value of the undersigned's home and household effects) of at least $250,000; or (ii) has a net worth of at least $250,000 (excluding home and household) and estimates that he/she will be in a 15 percent or more income tax bracket, on the basis of total federal income taxes for 2004. Furthermore, the undersigned represents and warrants that he/she has either (i) had experience in business enterprises or investments entailing risks of a type or to a degree substantially similar to those entailed in an investment in the company; or (ii) has obtained independent financial advice with respect to his/her investment in the units. The undersigned acknowledges receipt of a copy of the offering circular and represents and warrants that he/she is familiar with the offering circular and is aware of the risks involved in making an investment in the units.

The undersigned understands and agrees that this subscription is made subject to the following terms and conditions:

(a) The General Partner shall have the right to accept or reject this subscription, in whole or in part.

(b) The Limited Partnership Agreement to be issued and delivered based upon this subscription will only be issued in the name of, and delivered to, the undersigned. The undersigned also represents that the units to which they subscribe are not being purchased for subdivision or fictionalization and are solely for the account of the undersigned.

The undersigned constitutes and appoints James E. Glasgow Sr, with power of substitution, his/her attorney-in-fact for the purpose of executing and delivering on behalf of the undersigned the Limited Partnership Agreement between the undersigned and the other persons and parties who (together with the undersigned) shall constitute the partners of the company, and for the further purpose of executing and filing, on behalf of the undersigned, any and all Certificates of Limited Partnership required in order that the undersigned may obtain the benefits provided under the Uniform Limited Partnership Act of the state of Texas.

Dated _____, 2004

X_____
Signature

_____

Name [Print]

Married _____   Single _____
Address _____
City _____ State _____ Zip _____
Social Security Number _____
Domicile (if different from residence listed above)

_____

Appendix D

SAMPLE REFERRAL FORM

Referral Form

To: [General Partner]
Fax:

From: [Sender]

Please send an investment packet to the following potential Investors, who have requested I have one sent to them.

Name:
Address:
City, State, Zip:

Name:
Address:
City, State, Zip:

Name:
Address:
City, State, Zip:

Name:
Address:
City, State, Zip:

Signature:
[Print your name and contact information]

Appendix E

SAMPLE GENERAL PARTNER'S RÉSUMÉ

[Name of GP]
[Address]
[City, State, Zip]
Tel:
Fax:
E-mail:

Summary of Qualifications:

- 25 years' rental property ownership and management experience

- 20 years' experience in manufacturing and sales of storage buildings (owner and employee)

- 15 years' experience in retail store management

- 9 years' experience in sales management

- 17 years' business ownership and management experience

- 35 years' P&L (profit & loss) responsibility (owner and employee)

Professional and Employment Experience:

- 1987–present: Founder, President and CEO of Horizon Building System, DBA Patiostore.com, 3419 Northeast Parkway, San Antonio, TX 78218

Originally a manufacturer and retailer of portable buildings, the company was converted to a retailer of products for the backyard in the early 1990s. With the advent of the Internet, the company was transformed into an online retailer of our products including: aboveground pools, patio furniture, grills, home improvements, etc. We now have twelve (12) retail websites, including the parent website, www.patiostore.com. Sales average approximately $2.2 million.

- 1978–1987: District Sales Manager, Morgan Portable Buildings. My territory included 17 sales offices and three manufacturing plants across Texas, Arizona, and Colorado. Annual sales $6 million. I left this position to start my current company.

- 1976–1978: District Merchandise Manager, Globe Discount Stores. I was responsible for a 10-store district across Texas and Arizona with sales of $28 million. My responsibilities included sales volume, merchandise display, staff development, inventory control, and P&L goals. I left when the company, a division of Walgreen's Corp., dissolved.

- 1974-1976: Soft-Lines Manager, Globe Discount Stores San Antonio, Texas. My responsibilities included P&L, payroll control, staffing, training, inventory, sales, profitability, advertising and promotions.

- 1966-1973: Store manager, Perry Brothers Variety Store. Starting as Assistant Manager at age 17, I was promoted to store manager at age 20. I left to start a restaurant business.

Education

[List degree, university, graduation year]

Additional Coursework: Bee County College, 1968, course work in computers.

Ongoing Education: Numerous workshops, courses and classes over 25 years including but not limited to courses covering dynamic communications, bookkeeping, drafting & design of buildings, estimating, sales management, retail display, marketing, business legal, computer software, Internet marketing, business management, personal management, real estate sales, and investment management.

Experienced Instructor: I have and do give training classes covering: drafting & design of relocatable buildings, e-commerce and website design, small business management, salesmanship, and office management.

References: Available upon request

Appendix F

*PROPERTY EVALUATION FORM***

Address:		Property Type:	

Purchase price	
Estimated improvement cost	
Total estimated investment	

INCOME	Monthly	Annual
Estimated income		
Property taxes		
Insurance		
5% maintenance allowance		
Total operating cost		
Net operating income		

Property value

After rehab	
10% cap rate (net annual income x 10)	
Property value based on comps	
Monthly rent x 100	
(Single-family and duplexes only)	
Amount to refinance (66% of value)	

263

Cash Flow

$ Monthly	$ Annually	% Annually*

*On all cash deal: cash flow ÷ cash invested; with financing, cash flow – mortgage payments ÷ cash invested

**See chapter 16 for a sample of a completed form.

CPSIA information can be obtained at www.ICGtesting.com
Printed in the USA
BVOW11s2006290514

354713BV00011B/441/P